D0205560

THE SCHOMBURG LIBRARY OF
NINETEENTH-CENTURY BLACK WOMEN WRITERS

General Editor, Henry Louis Gates, Jr.

Titles are listed chronologically; collections that include works published over a span of years are listed according to the publication date of their initial work.

173113

The House of Bondage

or

Charlotte Brooks
and Other Slaves

OCTAVIA V. ROGERS ALBERT

With an Introduction by
FRANCES SMITH FOSTER

❧ ❧ ❧

973.0496
A333

❧ ❧ ❧

New York   Oxford
OXFORD UNIVERSITY PRESS
1988

Alverno College
Library Media Center
Milwaukee, Wisconsin

Oxford University Press

Oxford   New York   Toronto
Delhi   Bombay   Calcutta   Madras   Karachi
Petaling Jaya   Singapore   Hong Kong   Tokyo
Nairobi   Dar es Salaam   Cape Town
Melbourne   Auckland

and associated companies in
Beirut   Berlin   Ibadan   Nicosia

Copyright © 1988 by Oxford University Press, Inc.

Published by Oxford University Press, Inc.,
200 Madison Avenue, New York, New York 10016

Oxford is a registered trademark of Oxford University Press

All rights reserved. No part of this publication may be reproduced,
stored in a retrieval system, or transmitted, in any form or by any
means, electronic, mechanical, photocopying, recording, or otherwise,
without prior permission of Oxford University Press.

Library of Congress Cataloging-in-Publication Data

Albert, Octavia V. Rogers (Octavia Victoria Rogers),
1853–1889?
The house of bondage: or Charlotte Brooks and
other slaves.
(The Schomburg library of nineteenth-century black
women writers)
Originally published: c.1890.
1. Albert, Octavia V. Rogers (Octavia Victoria
Rogers), 1853–1889?   2. Slaves—United States—Biography.
3. Slavery—United States—Condition of slaves.
I. Title.   II. Title: House of bondage.   III. Title:
Charlotte Brooks and other slaves.   IV. Series.
E444.A33A3   1988   305.5'67'0973   87-24707
ISBN 0-19-505263-3
ISBN 0-19-505267-6 (set)
2 4 6 8 10 9 7 5 3 1

Printed in the United States of America
on acid-free paper

The
Schomburg Library
of
Nineteenth-Century
Black Women Writers
is
Dedicated
in Memory
of
PAULINE AUGUSTA COLEMAN GATES

1916–1987

PUBLISHER'S NOTE

Whenever possible, the volumes in this set were reproduced directly from original materials. When availability, physical condition of original texts, or other circumstances prohibited this, volumes or portions of volumes were reset.

FOREWORD
In Her Own Write

Henry Louis Gates, Jr.

One muffled strain in the Silent South, a jarring chord and a vague and uncomprehended cadenza has been and still is the Negro. And of that muffled chord, the one mute and voiceless note has been the sadly expectant Black Woman, ...

The "other side" has not been represented by one who "lives there." And not many can more sensibly realize and more accurately tell the weight and the fret of the "long dull pain" than the open-eyed but hitherto voiceless Black Woman of America.

. . . as our Caucasian barristers are not to blame if they cannot *quite* put themselves in the dark man's place, neither should the dark man be wholly expected fully and adequately to reproduce the exact Voice of the Black Woman.

—Anna Julia Cooper, *A Voice From the South* (1892)

The birth of the Afro-American literary tradition occurred in 1773, when Phillis Wheatley published a book of poetry. Despite the fact that her book garnered for her a remarkable amount of attention, Wheatley's journey to the printer had been a most arduous one. Sometime in 1772, a young African girl walked demurely into a room in Boston to undergo an oral examination, the results of which would determine the direction of her life and work. Perhaps she was shocked upon entering the appointed room. For there, perhaps gathered in a semicircle, sat eighteen of Boston's most notable citizens. Among them were John Erving, a prominent Boston merchant; the Reverend Charles Chauncy, pastor of the Tenth Congregational Church; and John Hancock, who would later gain fame for his signature on the Declaration of Independence. At the center of this group was His Excellency, Thomas Hutchinson, governor of Massachusetts, with Andrew Oliver, his lieutenant governor, close by his side.

Why had this august group been assembled? Why had it seen fit to summon this young African girl, scarcely eighteen years old, before it? This group of "the most respectable Characters in *Boston*," as it would later define itself, had assembled to question closely the African adolescent on the slender sheaf of poems that she claimed to have "written by herself." We can only speculate on the nature of the questions posed to the fledgling poet. Perhaps they asked her to identify and explain—for all to hear—exactly who were the Greek and Latin gods and poets alluded to so frequently in her work. Perhaps they asked her to conjugate a verb in Latin or even to translate randomly selected passages from the Latin, which she and her master, John Wheatley, claimed that she "had made some Progress in." Or perhaps they asked her to recite from memory key passages from the texts of John Milton and Alexander Pope, the two poets by whom the African claimed to be most directly influenced. We do not know.

We do know, however, that the African poet's responses were more than sufficient to prompt the eighteen august gentlemen to compose, sign, and publish a two-paragraph "Attestation," an open letter "To the Publick" that prefaces Phillis Wheatley's book and that reads in part:

> We whose Names are under-written, do assure the World, that the Poems specified in the following Page, were (as we

verily believe) written by Phillis, a young Negro Girl, who was but a few Years since, brought an uncultivated Barbarian from *Africa*, and has ever since been, and now is, under the Disadvantage of serving as a Slave in a Family in this Town. She has been examined by some of the best Judges, and is thought qualified to write them.

So important was this document in securing a publisher for Wheatley's poems that it forms the signal element in the prefatory matter preceding her *Poems on Various Subjects, Religious and Moral*, published in London in 1773.

Without the published "Attestation," Wheatley's publisher claimed, few would believe that an African could possibly have written poetry all by herself. As the eighteen put the matter clearly in their letter, "Numbers would be ready to suspect they were not really the Writings of Phillis." Wheatley and her master, John Wheatley, had attempted to publish a similar volume in 1772 in Boston, but Boston publishers had been incredulous. One year later, "Attestation" in hand, Phillis Wheatley and her master's son, Nathaniel Wheatley, sailed for England, where they completed arrangements for the publication of a volume of her poems with the aid of the Countess of Huntington and the Earl of Dartmouth.

This curious anecdote, surely one of the oddest oral examinations on record, is only a tiny part of a larger, and even more curious, episode in the Enlightenment. Since the beginning of the sixteenth century, Europeans had wondered aloud whether or not the African "species of men," as they were most commonly called, *could* ever create formal literature, could ever master "the arts and sciences." If they could, the argument ran, then the African variety of humanity was fundamentally related to the European variety. If not, then it seemed clear that the African was destined by nature

to be a slave. This was the burden shouldered by Phillis
Wheatley when she successfully defended herself and the au-
thorship of her book against counterclaims and doubts.

Indeed, with her successful defense, Wheatley launched
two traditions at once—the black American literary tradition
and the black woman's literary tradition. If it is extraordinary
that not just one but both of these traditions were founded
simultaneously by a black woman—certainly an event unique
in the history of literature—it is also ironic that this important fact of common, coterminous literary origins seems to
have escaped most scholars.

That the progenitor of the black literary tradition was a
woman means, in the most strictly literal sense, that all subsequent black writers have evolved in a matrilinear line of
descent, and that each, consciously or unconsciously, has extended and revised a canon whose foundation was the poetry
of a black woman. Early black writers seem to have been
keenly aware of Wheatley's founding role, even if most of
her white reviewers were more concerned with the implica-
tions of her race than her gender. Jupiter Hammon, for example, whose 1760 broadside "An Evening Thought. Salvation by Christ, With Penitential Cries" was the first
individual poem published by a black American, acknowl-
edged Wheatley's influence by selecting her as the subject of
his second broadside, "An Address to Miss Phillis Wheatly
[*sic*], Ethiopian Poetess, in Boston," which was published at
Hartford in 1778. And George Moses Horton, the second
Afro-American to publish a book of poetry in English (1829),
brought out in 1838 an edition of his *Poems By A Slave*
bound together with Wheatley's work. Indeed, for fifty-six
years, between 1773 and 1829, when Horton published *The
Hope of Liberty*, Wheatley was the *only* black person to have
published a book of imaginative literature in English. So

central was this black woman's role in the shaping of the
Afro-American literary tradition that, as one historian has
maintained, the history of the reception of Phillis Wheatley's
poetry *is* the history of Afro-American literary criticism. Well
into the nineteenth century, Wheatley and the black literary
tradition were the same entity.

But Wheatley is not the only black woman writer who
stands as a pioneering figure in Afro-American literature.
Just as Wheatley gave birth to the genre of black poetry, Ann
Plato was the first Afro-American to publish a book of essays
(1841) and Harriet E. Wilson was the first black person to
publish a novel in the United States (1859).

Despite this pioneering role of black women in the tradition, however, many of their contributions before this century have been all but lost or unrecognized. As Hortense
Spillers observed as recently as 1983,

> With the exception of a handful of autobiographical narratives
> from the nineteenth century, the black woman's realities are
> virtually suppressed until the period of the Harlem Renais-
> sance and later. Essentially the black woman as artist, as
> intellectual spokesperson for her own cultural apprenticeship,
> has not existed before, for anyone. At the source of [their]
> own symbol-making task, [the community of black women
> writers] confronts, therefore, a tradition of work that is quite
> recent, its continuities, broken and sporadic.

Until now, it has been extraordinarily difficult to establish
the formal connections between early black women's writing
and that of the present, precisely because our knowledge of
their work has been broken and sporadic. Phillis Wheatley,
for example, while certainly the most reprinted and discussed
poet in the tradition, is also one of the least understood. Ann
Plato's seminal work, *Essays* (which includes biographies and
poems), has not been reprinted since it was published a cen-

tury and a half ago. And Harriet Wilson's *Our Nig,* her compelling novel of a black woman's expanding consciousness in a racist Northern antebellum environment, never received even *one* review or comment at a time when virtually *all* works written by black people were heralded by abolitionists as salient arguments against the existence of human slavery. Many of the books reprinted in this set experienced a similar fate, the most dreadful fate for an author: that of being ignored then relegated to the obscurity of the rare book section of a university library. We can only wonder how many other texts in the black woman's tradition have been lost to this generation of readers or remain unclassified or uncatalogued and, hence, unread.

This was not always so, however. Black women writers dominated the final decade of the nineteenth century, perhaps spurred to publish by an 1886 essay entitled "The Coming American Novelist," which was published in *Lippincott's Monthly Magazine* and written by "A Lady From Philadelphia." This pseudonymous essay argued that the "Great American Novel" would be written by a black person. Her argument is so curious that it deserves to be repeated:

> When we come to formulate our demands of the Coming American Novelist, we will agree that he must be native-born. His ancestors may come from where they will, but we must give him a birthplace and have the raising of him. Still, the longer his family has been here the better he will represent us. Suppose he should have no country but ours, no traditions but those he has learned here, no longings apart from us, no future except in our future—the orphan of the world, he finds with us his home. And with all this, suppose he refuses to be fused into that grand conglomerate we call the "American type." With us, he is not of us. He is original, he has humor, he is tender, he is passive and fiery, he has been

taught what we call justice, and he has his own opinion about it. He has suffered everything a poet, a dramatist, a novelist need suffer before he comes to have his lips anointed. And with it all he is in one sense a spectator, a little out of the race. How would these conditions go towards forming an original development? In a word, suppose the coming novelist is of African origin? When one comes to consider the subject, there is no improbability in it. One thing is certain,—our great novel will not be written by the typical American.

An atypical American, indeed. Not only would the great American novel be written by an African-American, it would be written by an African-American *woman:*

> Yet farther: I have used the generic masculine pronoun because it is convenient; but Fate keeps revenge in store. It was a woman who, taking the wrongs of the African as her theme, wrote the novel that awakened the world to their reality, and why should not the coming novelist be a woman as well as an African? She—the woman of that race—has some claims on Fate which are not yet paid up.

It is these claims on fate that we seek to pay by publishing The Schomburg Library of Nineteenth-Century Black Women Writers.

This theme would be repeated by several black women authors, most notably by Anna Julia Cooper, a prototypical black feminist whose 1892 *A Voice From the South* can be considered to be one of the original texts of the black feminist movement. It was Cooper who first analyzed the fallacy of referring to "the Black man" when speaking of black people and who argued that just as white men cannot speak through the consciousness of black men, neither can black *men* "fully and adequately . . . reproduce the exact Voice of the Black Woman." Gender and race, she argues, cannot be conflated, except in the instance of a black woman's voice, and it is this voice which must be uttered and to which we must listen. As Cooper puts the matter so compellingly:

> It is not the intelligent woman vs. the ignorant woman; nor the white woman vs. the black, the brown, and the red,—it is not even the cause of woman vs. man. Nay, 'tis woman's strongest vindication for speaking that *the world needs to hear her voice*. It would be subversive of every human interest that the cry of one-half the human family be stifled. Woman in stepping from the pedestal of statue-like inactivity in the domestic shrine, and daring to think and move and speak,— to undertake to help shape, mold, and direct the thought of her age, is merely completing the circle *of* the world's vision. Hers is every interest that has lacked an interpreter and a defender. Her cause is linked with that of every agony that has been dumb—every wrong that needs a voice.
>
> It is no fault of man's that he has not been able to see truth from her standpoint. It does credit both to his head and heart that no greater mistakes have been committed or even wrongs perpetrated while she sat making tatting and snipping paper flowers. Man's own innate chivalry and the mutual interdependence of their interests have insured his treating her cause, in the main at least, as his own. And he is pardonably surprised and even a little chagrined, perhaps, to find his legislation not considered "perfectly lovely" in every respect. But in any case his work is only impoverished by her remaining dumb. The world has had to limp along with the wobbling gait and one-sided hesitancy of a man with one eye. Suddenly the bandage is removed from the other eye and the whole body is filled with light. It sees a circle where before it saw a segment. The darkened eye restored, every member rejoices with it.

The myopic sight of the darkened eye can only be restored when the full range of the black woman's voice, with its own special timbres and shadings, remains mute no longer.

Similarly, Victoria Earle Matthews, an author of short stories and essays, and a cofounder in 1896 of the National Association of Colored Women, wrote in her stunning essay, "The Value of Race Literature" (1895), that "when the literature of our race is developed, it will of necessity be different in all essential points of greatness, true heroism and real Christianity from what we may at the present time, for convenience, call American literature." Matthews argued that this great tradition of Afro-American literature would be the textual outlet "for the unnaturally suppressed inner lives which our people have been compelled to lead." Once these "unnaturally suppressed inner lives" of black people are unveiled, no "grander diffusion of mental light" will shine more brightly, she concludes, than that of the articulate Afro-American woman:

And now comes the question, What part shall we women play in the Race Literature of the future? . . . within the compass of one small journal ["Woman's Era"] we have struck out a new line of departure—a journal, a record of Race interests gathered from all parts of the United States, carefully selected, moistened, winnowed and garnered by the ablest intellects of educated colored women, shrinking at no lofty theme, shirking no serious duty, aiming at every possible excellence, and determined to do their part in the future uplifting of the race.

If twenty women, by their concentrated efforts in one literary movement, can meet with such success as has engendered, planned out, and so successfully consummated this convention, what much more glorious results, what wider spread success, what grander diffusion of mental light will not come forth at the bidding of the enlarged hosts of women writers, already called into being by the stimulus of your efforts?

And here let me speak one word for my journalistic sisters

who have already entered the broad arena of journalism. Before the "Woman's Era" had come into existence, no one except themselves can appreciate the bitter experience and sore disappointments under which they have at all times been compelled to pursue their chosen vocations.

If their brothers of the press have had their difficulties to contend with, I am here as a sister journalist to state, from the fullness of knowledge, that their task has been an easy one compared with that of the colored woman in journalism.

Woman's part in Race Literature, as in Race building, is the most important part and has been so in all ages. . . . All through the most remote epochs she has done her share in literature. . . .

One of the most important aspects of this set is the republication of the salient texts from 1890 to 1910, which literary historians could well call "The Black Woman's Era." In addition to Mary Helen Washington's definitive edition of Cooper's *A Voice From the South,* we have reprinted two novels by Amelia Johnson, Frances Harper's *Iola Leroy,* two novels by Emma Dunham Kelley, Alice Dunbar-Nelson's two impressive collections of short stories, and Pauline Hopkins's three serialized novels as well as her monumental novel, *Contending Forces*—all published between 1890 and 1910. Indeed, black women published more works of fiction in these two decades than black men had published in the previous half century. Nevertheless, this great achievement has been ignored.

Moreover, the writings of nineteenth-century Afro-American women in general have remained buried in obscurity, accessible only in research libraries or in overpriced and poorly edited reprints. Many of these books have never been reprinted at all; in some instances only one or two copies are extant. In these works of fiction, poetry, autobiography, biography, essays, and journalism resides the mind of the nineteenth-century Afro-American woman. Until these works are made readily available to teachers and their students, a significant segment of the black tradition will remain silent.

Oxford University Press, in collaboration with the Schomburg Center for Research in Black Culture, is publishing thirty volumes of these compelling works, each of which contains an introduction by an expert in the field. The set includes such rare texts as Johnson's *The Hazeley Family* and *Clarence and Corinne*, Plato's *Essays*, the most complete edition of Phillis Wheatley's poems and letters, Emma Dunham Kelley's pioneering novel *Megda*, several previously unpublished stories and a novel by Alice Dunbar-Nelson, and the first collected volumes of Pauline Hopkins's three serialized novels and Frances Harper's poetry. We also present four volumes of poetry by such women as Mary Eliza Tucker Lambert, Adah Menken, Josephine Heard, and Maggie Johnson. Numerous slave and spiritual narratives, a newly discovered novel—*Four Girls at Cottage City*—by Emma Dunham Kelley (-Hawkins), and the first American edition of *Wonderful Adventures of Mrs. Seacole in Many Lands* are also among the texts included.

In addition to resurrecting the works of black women authors, it is our hope that this set will facilitate the resurrection of the Afro-American woman's literary tradition itself by unearthing its nineteenth-century roots. In the works of Nella Larsen and Jessie Fauset, Zora Neale Hurston and Ann Petry, Lorraine Hansberry and Gwendolyn Brooks, Paule Marshall and Toni Cade Bambara, Audre Lorde and Rita Dove, Toni Morrison and Alice Walker, Gloria Naylor and Jamaica Kincaid, these roots have branched luxuriantly. The eighteenth- and nineteenth-century authors whose works are presented in this set founded and nurtured the black women's literary tradition, which must be revived, explicated, analyzed, and debated before we can understand more completely the formal shaping of this tradition within a tradition, a coded literary universe through which, regrettably, we are only just beginning to navigate our way. As Anna Cooper said nearly one hundred years ago, we have been blinded by the loss of sight in one eye and have therefore been unable to detect the full *shape* of the Afro-American literary tradition.

Literary works configure into a tradition not because of some mystical collective unconscious determined by the biology of race or gender, but because writers read other writers and *ground* their representations of experience in models of language provided largely by other writers to whom they feel akin. It is through this mode of literary revision, amply evident in the *texts* themselves—in formal echoes, recast metaphors, even in parody—that a "tradition" emerges and defines itself.

This is formal bonding, and it is only through formal bonding that we can know a literary tradition. The collective publication of these works by black women now, for the first time, makes it possible for scholars and critics, male and female, black and white, to *demonstrate* that black women writers read, and revised, other black women writers. To demonstrate this set of formal literary relations is to demonstrate that sexuality, race, and gender are both the condition and the basis of *tradition*—but tradition as found in discrete acts of language use.

A word is in order about the history of this set. For the past decade, I have taught a course, first at Yale and then at Cornell, entitled "Black Women and Their Fictions," a course that I inherited from Toni Morrison, who developed it in the mid-1970s for Yale's Program in Afro-American Studies. Although the course was inspired by the remarkable accomplishments of black women novelists since 1970, I gradually extended its beginning date to the late nineteenth century, studying Frances Harper's *Iola Leroy* and Anna Julia Cooper's *A Voice From the South,* both published in 1892. With the discovery of Harriet E. Wilson's seminal novel, *Our Nig* (1859), and Jean Yellin's authentication of Harriet Jacobs's brilliant slave narrative, *Incidents in the Life of a Slave Girl* (1861), a survey course spanning over a century and a quarter emerged.

But the discovery of *Our Nig,* as well as the interest in nineteenth-century black women's writing that this discovery generated, convinced me that even the most curious and diligent scholars knew very little of the extensive history of the creative writings of Afro-American women before 1900. Indeed, most scholars of Afro-American literature had never even read most of the books published by black women, simply because these books—of poetry, novels, short stories, essays, and autobiography—were mostly accessible only in rare book sections of university libraries. For reasons unclear to me even today, few of these marvelous renderings of the Afro-American woman's consciousness were reprinted in the late 1960s and early 1970s, when so many other texts of the Afro-American literary tradition were resurrected from the dark and silent graveyard of the out-of-print and were reissued in facsimile editions aimed at the hungry readership for canonical texts in the nascent field of black studies.

So, with the help of several superb research assistants—including David Curtis, Nicola Shilliam, Wendy Jones, Sam Otter, Janadas Devan, Suvir Kaul, Cynthia Bond, Elizabeth Alexander, and Adele Alexander—and with the expert advice of scholars such as William Robinson, William Andrews, Mary Helen Washington, Maryemma Graham, Jean Yellin, Houston A. Baker, Jr., Richard Yarborough, Hazel Carby, Joan R. Sherman, Frances Foster, and William French, dozens of bibliographies were used to compile a list of books written or narrated by black women mostly before 1910. Without the assistance provided through this shared experience of scholarship, the scholar's true legacy, this project could not have been conceived. As the list grew, I was struck by how very many of these titles that I, for example, had never even heard of, let alone read, such as Ann Plato's *Essays*, Louisa Picquet's slave narrative, or Amelia Johnson's two novels, *Clarence and Corinne* and *The Hazeley Family*. Through our research with the Black Periodical Fiction and Poetry Project (funded by NEH and the Ford Foundation), I also realized that several novels by black women, including three works of fiction by Pauline Hopkins, had been serialized in black periodicals, but had never been collected and published as books. Nor had the several books of poetry published by black women, such as the prolific Frances E. W. Harper, been collected and edited. When I discovered still another "lost" novel by an Afro-American woman (*Four Girls at Cottage City*, published in 1898 by Emma Dunham Kelley-Hawkins), I decided to attempt to edit a collection of reprints of these works and to publish them as a "library" of black women's writings, in part so that I could read them myself.

Convincing university and trade publishers to undertake this project proved to be a difficult task. Despite the commercial success of *Our Nig* and of the several reprint series of women's works (such as Virago, the Beacon Black Women Writers Series, and Rutgers' American Women Writers Series), several presses rejected the project as "too large," "too limited," or as "commercially unviable." Only two publishers recognized the viability and the import of the project and, of these, Oxford's commitment to publish the titles simultaneously as a set made the press's offer irresistible.

While attempting to locate original copies of these exceedingly rare books, I discovered that most of the texts were housed at the Schomburg Center for Research in Black Culture, a branch of The New York Public Library, under the direction of Howard Dodson. Dodson's infectious enthusiasm for the project and his generous collaboration, as well as that of his stellar staff (especially Diana Lachatanere, Sharon Howard, Ellis Haizip, Richard Newman, and Betty Gubert), led to a joint publishing initiative that produced this set as part of the Schomburg's major fund-raising campaign. Without Dodson's foresight and generosity of spirit, the set would not have materialized. Without William P. Sisler's masterful editorship at Oxford and his staff's careful attention to detail, the set would have remained just another grand idea that tends to languish in a scholar's file cabinet.

I would also like to thank Dr. Michael Winston and Dr. Thomas C. Battle, Vice-President of Academic Affairs and the Director of the Moorland-Spingarn Research Center (respectively) at Howard University, for their unending encouragement, support, and collaboration in this project, and Esme E. Bhan at Howard for her meticulous research and bibliographical skills. In addition, I would like to acknowledge the aid of the staff at the libraries of Duke University, Cornell University (especially Tom Weissinger and Donald Eddy), the Boston Public Library, the Western Reserve Historical Society, the Library of Congress, and Yale University. Linda Robbins, Marion Osmun, Sarah Flanagan, and Gerard Case, all members of the staff at Oxford, were

extraordinarily effective at coordinating, editing, and producing the various segments of each text in the set. Candy
Ruck, Nina de Tar, and Phillis Molock expertly typed reams
of correspondence and manuscripts connected to the project.

I would also like to express my gratitude to my colleagues
who edited and introduced the individual titles in the set.
Without their attention to detail, their willingness to meet
strict deadlines, and their sheer enthusiasm for this project,
the set could not have been published. But finally and ulti-
mately, I would hope that the publication of the set would
help to generate even more scholarly interest in the black
women authors whose work is presented here. Struggling
against the seemingly insurmountable barriers of racism *and*
sexism, while often raising families and fulfilling full-time
professional obligations, these women managed nevertheless
to record their thoughts and feelings and to *testify* to all who
dare read them that the will to harness the power of collective
endurance and survival is the will to write.

The Schomburg Library of Nineteenth-Century Black
Women Writers is dedicated in memory of Pauline Augusta
Coleman Gates, who died in the spring of 1987. It was she
who inspired in me the love of learning and the love of literature. I have encountered in the books of this set no will
more determined, no courage more noble, no mind more
sublime, no self more celebratory of the achievements of all
Afro-American women, and indeed of life itself, than her
own.

A NOTE FROM
THE SCHOMBURG CENTER

Howard Dodson

The Schomburg Center for Research in Black Culture, The New York Public Library, is pleased to join with Dr. Henry Louis Gates and Oxford University Press in presenting The Schomburg Library of Nineteenth-Century Black Women Writers. This thirty-volume set includes the work of a generation of black women whose writing has only been available previously in rare book collections. The materials reprinted in twenty-four of the thirty volumes are drawn from the unique holdings of the Schomburg Center.

A research unit of The New York Public Library, the Schomburg Center has been in the forefront of those institutions dedicated to collecting, preserving, and providing access to the records of the black past. In the course of its two generations of acquisition and conservation activity, the Center has amassed collections totaling more than 5 million items. They include over 100,000 bound volumes, 85,000 reels and sets of microforms, 300 manuscript collections containing some 3.5 million items, 300,000 photographs and extensive holdings of prints, sound recordings, film and videotape, newspapers, artworks, artifacts, and other book and nonbook materials. Together they vividly document the history and cultural heritages of people of African descent worldwide.

Though established some sixty-two years ago, the Center's book collections date from the sixteenth century. Its oldest item, an Ethiopian Coptic Tunic, dates from the eighth or ninth century. Rare materials, however, are most available for the nineteenth-century African-American experience. It is from these holdings that the majority of the titles selected for inclusion in this set are drawn.

The nineteenth century was a formative period in African-American literary and cultural history. Prior to the Civil War, the majority of black Americans living in the United States were held in bondage. Law and practice forbade teaching them to read or write. Even after the war, many of the impediments to learning and literary productivity remained. Nevertheless, black men and women of the nineteenth century persevered in both areas. Moreover, more African-Americans than we yet realize turned their observations, feelings, social viewpoints, and creative impulses into published works. In time, this nineteenth-century printed record included poetry, short stories, histories, novels, autobiographies, social criticism, and theology, as well as economic and philosophical treatises. Unfortunately, much of this body of literature remained, until very recently, relatively inaccessible to twentieth-century scholars, teachers, creative artists, and others interested in black life. Prior to the late 1960s, most Americans (black as well as white) had never heard of these nineteenth-century authors, much less read their works.

The civil rights and black power movements created unprecedented interest in the thought, behavior, and achievements of black people. Publishers responded by revising traditional texts, introducing the American public to a new generation of African-American writers, publishing a variety of thematic anthologies, and reprinting a plethora of "classic texts" in African-American history, literature, and art. The reprints usually appeared as individual titles or in a series of bound volumes or microform formats.

The Schomburg Center, which has a long history of supporting publishing that deals with the history and culture of Africans in diaspora, became an active participant in many of the reprint revivals of the 1960s. Since hard copies of original printed works are the preferred formats for producing facsimile reproductions, publishers frequently turned to the Schomburg Center for copies of these original titles. In addition to providing such material, Schomburg Center staff members offered advice and consultation, wrote introductions, and occasionally entered into formal copublishing arrangements in some projects.

Most of the nineteenth-century titles reprinted during the 1960s, however, were by and about black men. A few black women were included in the longer series, but works by lesser known black women were generally overlooked. The Schomburg Library of Nineteenth-Century Black Women Writers is both a corrective to these previous omissions and an important contribution to Afro-American literary history in its own right. Through this collection of volumes, the thoughts, perspectives, and creative abilities of nineteenth-century African-American women, as captured in books and pamphlets published in large part before 1910, are again being made available to the general public. The Schomburg Center is pleased to be a part of this historic endeavor.

I would like to thank Professor Gates for initiating this project. Thanks are due both to him and Mr. William P. Sisler of Oxford University Press for giving the Schomburg Center an opportunity to play such a prominent role in the set. Thanks are also due to my colleagues at The New York Public Library and the Schomburg Center, especially Dr. Vartan Gregorian, Richard De Gennaro, Paul Fasana, Betsy

INTRODUCTION

Frances Smith Foster

Who shall return to tell Egypt the story . . . ?
———OCTAVIA V. ROGERS ALBERT, ca. 1890

What did it mean for a black woman to be an artist in our grandmothers' time? In our great-grandmothers' day? It is a question with an answer cruel enough to stop the blood.
———ALICE WALKER, 1974

The House of Bondage: or Charlotte Brooks and Other Slaves is a remarkable book with special appeal for modern readers. It is, first of all, a book about American slavery, a subject that continues to claim our interest and to excite our imaginations. Its narrator serves as an interpreter between us and those who participated in this experience, offering the immediacy of the first-person account mediated by a sensitivity to our particular questions and concerns. First published in 1890, the book is also an example of nineteenth-century literature, of nineteenth-century Afro-American literature, and of nineteenth-century Afro-American women's literature. As such it offers fascinating comparisons between our expectations and desires as readers and those of readers of almost a century ago and between its treatment of slavery and the treatment that topic received by popular nineteenth-century Anglo-American writers. Finally, it exemplifies some of the strategies that black women writers have adopted in response to racist and sexist expectations.

In her now classic essay, "In Search of Our Mothers' Gardens," Alice Walker articulated the question that an increasing number of people had been thinking about: What about the women who were not sisters of Shakespeare and had neither room nor body to call their own? What was the impact of sex and race upon the creative impulses of early Afro-American women writers? Walker concludes that while the situation for our artistic foremothers was one of blood-stopping cruelty, it is a mistake to believe that they produced no art. Then, as now, artists who were both black and female were severely debilitated by the coldly inhumane circumstances of their lives; nonetheless, some were able to survive and to express their talents by appropriating traditional forms, inventing new ones, and, quite often, by disguising their art as artlessness. Octavia Albert (1853–1890[?]) was one such artist.

Though she was a skilled writer, Albert wrote not simply to satisfy her artistic inclinations, but also to correct and to create history. In so doing she entered an intense competition to describe and design the material and moral fabric of an emerging society. Beginning with the premise that many written accounts of slavery were inaccurate and inadequate, Albert offered personal narratives of former slaves and her own commentary in order to supplement or to refute those accounts. The hymn that concludes Albert's volume summarizes her theme that abolition was the triumph of God's will over evil and that those who have been delivered must return to tell the story.

The story that *The House of Bondage* tells is an enthralling and personal one. Its depictions of life during and just after slavery personalize an era that today is almost an abstraction. The last of the witnesses to American slavery have died. For most of us, slavery is but a word, explained by other words, themselves barely understood: middle passage, chains, auction block. Slaves exist in the popular imagination as stereotypes: Uncle Tom, Aunt Jemima, or Kunta Kinte. Aunt Charlotte and her friends do not fit these modes. They are more human, more ordinary, more real. Their narratives make clear and concrete the meaning of slavery. Their heroism of enduring, of persevering, of keeping the faith is less dramatic but somehow more profound. They are more easily imagined as progenitors of our own immediate families.

The racial situation today is not much different from what it was when *The House of Bondage* was first published. Then, as now, the nation was in transition. The Civil War was over. Civil rights legislation was in place. Despite the failure of the Reconstruction, most people were eager to believe that with the help of right-thinking Anglo-Americans, Afro-Americans were making progress. They considered white supremacy groups to be a regrettable but understandable reaction to the radicalism of the carpetbag extremists, a backlash that they believed would dissipate in the forthcoming climate of progress and prosperity. Poised at the beginning of a new century, Americans had survived much and faced more. They preferred to focus on the promises of the future and to use only those elements from history that supported their aspirations.

Still, the twentieth century is not the nineteenth, and the significance of this work increases when viewed in the context of the time during which it first appeared. The reading public of the late nineteenth century included an entire generation of Americans who had come of age after slavery had ceased to be a legal institution in the United States. For them, that era was history. They, and most Americans who had not lived in the South, relied upon written accounts for their understanding of life under the peculiar institution. These readers favored the antebellum romances of Thomas Nelson Page over the disturbing realism of abolitionist narratives. They chose Uncle Remus over Uncle Tom as the prototypical slave. In the words of William Dean Howells, "The wrecks of slavery [were] fast growing a fungus crop of sentiment" (Hart, p. 202). James D. Hart summarized the literary preferences of that period in this way: "Social idealists continued to present new plans of protest and reform, but the larger body of readers, . . . preferred novels reflecting the standards that had brought success or stories that granted surcease from the troubled times. . . . Whatever the subject, the mood was predominantly one of escape and the medium one of romance" (p. 200).

Octavia Victoria Rogers Albert was one of those social idealists who protested literary misrepresentation of both the recent slave past and the present condition of the former slaves. She knew that slavery had been far more insidious than popular literature portrayed and that, while a black middle class was struggling into existence, the masses of former slaves lived in abject poverty. Albert asserted that millions of Afro-Americans were suffering from illiteracy, unemployment, and chronic illnesses, that their moral standing was "far from what it should be," and that this situation was a direct result of slavery.

Her plan for reform rested upon a sober recognition of this shameful heritage and upon each individual's prayerful acceptance of responsibility for its legacies and its lessons. Slavery had flourished in a Christian nation, and that nation was obliged to understand clearly the nature of the sin it had nurtured. National progress and, more importantly, the salvation of its people required repentance and atonement. True Christians, Albert believed, could not "sit quietly by and see the needs of seven millions or more of human souls crying in the valley of sin and sorrow and not give a listening ear to them" (p. 58).

Octavia Albert first lived her convictions as a teacher in rural Georgia. When she married the Reverend A. E. P. Albert and moved to Houma, Louisiana, her home became a gathering place for former slaves. There she offered them food, read them scriptures, taught them to read and write, and encouraged them to talk about themselves and their slave experiences. Such activities were not particularly unusual for a college-educated minister's wife. Her status in that rural Southern area allowed, even expected, such compassion. However, her decision to provide more than a listening ear, to become their voice as well, surprised even her informants. Upon learning Albert's intention to record the personal histories of former slaves, Aunt Charlotte responded, "La, me, child! I never thought any body would care enough for me to tell of my trials and sorrows in this world!" (p. 27). This reaction implies more than personal modesty. Despite the swirling controversy over the nature of American slavery and the future of its newly emancipated citizens, both women knew that few bothered to consider the slaves' views.

Octavia Albert's motivations went beyond her strong religious convictions. She had been born before the war to slave parents. Although she was therefore a former slave herself, Emancipation had come before she fully realized her condition. Understanding slavery was for her a way of discovering herself. Since she was new to Louisiana, unrelated to the informants, eager to learn about the state's particular manifestations of slavery, but well acquainted with the subject generally, she was a knowledgeable, sympathetic, but relatively objective investigator. Most importantly, Albert had studied at Atlanta University and was, according to historian John Blassingame, one of the "few well-trained interviewers" in the country (p. lxi). As a nineteenth-century black woman, she had few outlets for her academic training, civic interests, or personal creativity. This project, however, could be done at home, with discretion and in the name of the Lord.

It is probable that when she began her interviews, neither she nor her informants expected these oral histories to be published beyond their circle of family and friends. In the 1870s, whatever was published by Afro-Americans was published primarily by men. The first interviews resemble the antebellum slave narratives in their depictions of cruel punishments, divided families, and debilitating labor. To these almost stock images, Albert added information about religious beliefs and practices. She emphasized particularly the trials and tribulations of Protestant slaves in a Catholic region. As the years progressed, Albert's focus moved to the condition and progress of the former slaves. The final chapters describe occasions in 1884 and 1888 during which she and other members of the talented tenth demonstrated their cultural and material achievements. Over the years Albert's mission had changed from interviewing friends and neighbors to becoming a public advocate for social change.

It was an audacious act for a nineteenth-century woman to presume to address any audience outside her own family and female friends. There was definitely a woman's sphere, and those who wrote for publication were dangerously close to exceeding its bounds. As Cheryl Walker says in *The Night-*

ingale's Burden: Women Poets and American Culture Before 1900, "it was still obvious to many women that they were doing something not quite feminine in entering the literary world" (p. 34). Though women novelists had achieved some degree of acceptance, it was a tenuous and highly qualified position. By and large they wrote to female audiences, limited their subjects largely to hearth and home, and confined their advice to advocating "duty, discipline, self-control, and sacrifice" (Baym, p. 18). The few, such as Harriet Beecher Stowe or Helen Hunt Jackson, who took on larger issues or engaged in social debate were viciously attacked for having "unsexed" themselves.

This was particularly problematic for the Afro-American middle class, which so strongly desired the social approval and respect of their fellow Americans and so consistently received neither. For a black woman to address an audience of mixed race and sex, to accuse her readers of having sinned by commission or omission, and to urge their active involvement in social and political reform was to risk being totally rejected as an iconoclast or a lunatic. Perhaps this is why Albert's work was not published until after her death and why the work is prefaced by three separate testimonies that emphasize her "angelic spirit" and her "pure and consecrated life." In presenting Albert's work to the reading public, they herald the author as a "devoted mother and wife," and they recommend her work for its ability to "cheer and comfort and inspire to high and holy deeds." They focus the reader's attention away from the audacity of a black woman writer and upon the authenticity of the narratives and the sacredness of the endeavor.

Since Octavia Albert was both a committed Christian and a serious scholar, these eulogistic prefaces do not violate the integrity of her text, but they are in marked contrast with her tone. The narrator of *The House of Bondage*, often addressed by her informants as "Mrs. A.," is assertive, even strident. Like many of the Puritans, the slave narrators, and other women writers, Albert frequently refers to the Bible for both her conclusions and her right to voice them. This technique, which had become standard for persuasive literature, does recognize the possible objections to her writing, but rejects them by evoking a higher authority than social convention. It was, she declared, her Christian duty to follow the Biblical dictates to "Cry aloud, spare not, lift up thy voice like a trumpet, and show my people their transgression" (p. 85). It had been, she maintained, the refusal of others to lift their voices that had exacerbated the sins of the few and left them all in danger of divine retribution. Although the slave masters were to blame for the brutality of slavery, Albert believed that the entire nation would be held accountable to God for allowing slavery to continue so long. It was, she declared, an era that the Spanish Inquisition could hardly rival for infamy.

The narratives that comprise *The House of Bondage* were first published as a series of articles in the *South-western Christian Advocate* from January to December 1890. This was a good marriage of medium and message. The *Advocate* was owned by the General Conference of the Methodist Episcopal Church and had the largest circulation of any paper in New Orleans. It was the only such periodical to have an Afro-American editor and to count among its subscribers "thousands" of white readers (Penn, p. 226). In the post-Reconstruction days of its publication, it was likely that a good number of *Advocate* readers were, as Albert had been, relatively new to the area and had little or no direct experience with slavery as it existed in Louisiana. Nonetheless, most of the readers were undoubtedly Southerners, and few would have been indifferent to the legacies of slavery and the questions concerning the future of the former slaves. Like Albert, many of the *Advocate's* readers believed a theology of social action. They would agree with Uncle Cephas, one of her narrators, who maintained that "Education, property, and character, to my mind, have ever been the trinity of power to which I have looked and do look for our complete redemption in this country" (p. 127). Consequently, it is easy to believe the book's initial preface, which claims that the series was being published in volume form (in late 1890) by popular demand.

But despite its strong Protestantism and the fact that it was first published in a church-sponsored periodical, *The House of Bondage* is not merely the pious exhortations of an emboldened female evangelist. It is sectarian and secularly political. In comparing American slavery to the Spanish Inquisition, Albert was making, as her contemporaries would certainly have recognized, an extremely harsh indictment. Catholicism was never a particularly popular religion in the United States. And in Louisiana, her readers shared her distaste for Papist politics. With her anti-Catholic tenor, Albert claims the priority of Protestantism over race. She charges Catholic slaveholders with additional guilt because to human oppression they added religious fraud and persecution. A frequent refrain in the narratives of Albert's informants is the difficulty of practicing their faith when owned by Catholics. Their litany of abuses include being forced to work on Sunday, being refused permission to attend church or to sing hymns, and being unable to convince slaves born into Catholic households to abandon their "beads and crosses."

To believe that this publication was intended as nothing more than "a memorial of the author" and "a history of negro slavery" (p. v) would also be a mistake. The project may have begun as a personal mission, but by the time the essays were collected in volume form, they were intended to influence public opinion and policy on a national scale. Not only was *The House of Bondage* jointly published in New York and Cincinnati, but according to prominent theologian and social activist Bishop Willard F. Mallalieu, it was addressed to a diverse audience. Mallalieu declared that the book would refute those inclined to excuse American slavery as having been "of divine appointment"; it would remind Americans of the "depths of disgrace and infamy" from which abolition had raised them; and it would show Afro-Americans in particular that their delivery from a bondage "worse than Egyptian" was by "the exceeding mercy of God" (pp. xii–xiii).

Octavia Albert may have made no special efforts to claim literary merit, but she does use literary techniques common to fiction and poetry. She uses dialogue, and she experiments with dialect. She responds to current interest in local color and regional diversity with description and commentary. She incorporates songs and poems within her text. She appeals to the reader's emotions, interrupts the narrative to address the audience directly, and adopts a narrative persona that is slightly autobiographical but also consciously created to elicit a particular reader response.

Albert obviously was a well-read individual and her book, which is a carefully crafted venture, displays the influence of several genres. She explicitly compares Aunt Charlotte's story with that of Bunyan's *Pilgrim's Progress*. She relates the bondage and freedom experiences of her informants not only in accordance with the Judeo-Christian concepts of Divine Providence but also in terms that echo the Indian Captivity tales of eighteenth-century New England. In its emphasis on the institution of slavery and its use of individual accounts as examples of slave life, Albert's work resembles most antebellum slave narratives. And in form and theology, it is strikingly similar to group biographies such as Benjamin Drew's *A North-Side View of Slavery* and William Wells Brown's *My Southern Home*. *The House of Bondage* may even be seen as the literary sequel to Brown's *Panoramic Views of the Scenes in the Life of an American Slave.*

As the writing of a nineteenth-century, middle-class Afro-American, *The House of Bondage* reveals significant differences between the racial attitudes of blacks and whites. Comparing Albert's writing about slavery to Anglo-American literature about slavery is particularly instructive. Octavia Albert's depiction of slavery and its aftermath is in clear contrast to the two most popular nineteenth-century authorities, Harriet Beecher Stowe and Thomas Nelson Page.

Both Octavia Albert and Harriet Stowe were evangelists of a social theology, preaching a gospel of spiritual development as the sure way to earthly prosperity. Indeed, the subtitle of *Uncle Tom's Cabin—Life Among the Lowly*—could have followed *The House of Bondage* as well, for Albert, like Stowe, presents herself as an interpreter of a culture that is a part of, but obviously inferior to, that shared by her readers and herself. Both writers challenge their readers to live their religious faith by recognizing their common bond with the more oppressed members of the Christian family. Their works emphasize the unshakable Christian faith of the slaves who survived their captivity despite the ridicule, unbelief, or hypocrisy of their masters. Both compare slavery in the

United States to the Egyptian bondage of the children of Israel, and both indict Americans more strongly because slavery took place in a nation they considered both civilized and Christian. The conclusion to *Uncle Tom's Cabin* reads much like Albert's introduction when Stowe says: "Both North and South have been guilty before God; and the *Christian Church* has a heavy account to answer" (p. 476). And she, too, declares that what she writes is but "a faint shadow, a dim picture, of the anguish and despair" of slavery (p. 471).

On the other hand, Albert differs most significantly from Stowe in her depiction of characters and her visions of a free future. During their enslavement, Aunt Charlotte and her friends were indeed long suffering. But unlike Stowe's characters, they did not resort to humorous subterfuge, and they were not always passive. They fed and sheltered fugitive slaves, they disobeyed direct orders, and they sometimes went so far as to hit back when unjustly punished. Whereas Stowe's Uncle Tom was such a paragon of truth and virtue that he would admit knowing details of an escape but accept a fatal beating rather than tell them to his master, several of Albert's characters found their Christian beliefs no hindrance to betraying their masters' confidence. They vehemently asserted personal indifference to earthly freedom when in fact such assurances were tactics to ensure the success of their escapes.

Nor does Albert share Stowe's racism. She gives few details of color and facial features and does not assign the highest intellect and the greatest insight to mulatto characters. Whereas Stowe could not bring herself to imagine an integrated society and therefore offers her characters freedom only in heaven or in Africa, Albert believed that blacks could, should, and would take their rightful places as citizens in the United States.

Such comparisons were not lost on Afro-Americans such as Monroe Majors, who wrote in 1893 that

> between Mrs. Stowe's "Uncle Tom's Cabin" and Mrs. Al-
> bert's "House of Bondage" there is a most beautiful contrast;
> the former dignifies the Negro as a fugitive and asserts his
> rights to be a fugitive; the latter shows up the unrelenting
> patience of the Negro and his unrivaled faith in the Giver of
> all good. Again, the former is scenic, presenting a most
> beautiful as well as lasting, yet touching landscape; while the
> latter is just what its title identifies—"The House of Bon-
> dage." (p. 227)

As Majors' analysis shows, *The House of Bondage* was not considered a refutation of *Uncle Tom's Cabin* as much as it was interpreted as a complement or a sequel. Yet, if one insists on choosing which version is most authentic, the opening sentence of Albert's first chapter declares the priority of her accounts over the reports of any, including Harriet Stowe, who wrote of the South without having lived there. Says Albert, "None but those who resided in the South during the time of slavery can realize the terrible punishments that were visited upon the slaves" (p. 1). With this statement, she does not directly assert her personal authority over that of others; rather, she proclaims the priority of personal experience over sympathetic imagination.

With Thomas Nelson Page, the situation is different. Page was a leading practitioner of the Plantation School, that group of writers who created the romantic notion of the antebellum South as a series of stately mansions, rustling crinolines, and grinning darkies. Albert's version of the slave South seems consciously designed as a direct challenge to that notion. Her title, *The House of Bondage: or Charlotte Brooks and Other Slaves,* is quite similar to that of Page's *In Ole Virginia; Or,*

Marsh Chan and Other Stories, which had been published three years earlier. *In Ole Virginia* is also a collection of narratives told by a stranger to the antebellum South. Page's narrator comes upon a group of people living in an area of rural Virginia oblivious to "the outer world which strode by them as they dreamed" (p. 1). Page's characters are primarily former house slaves who mourn the passing of antebellum aristocracy, chivalry, and romance. Their narratives are more about their masters' experiences than their own. Albert's informants, however, talk of their feelings and activities as workers on relatively small farms or in the urban areas. They are not the faithful retainers of an imagined aristocracy but rather the typical exploited beings who served the struggling majority that composed the slaveholder class. Like Page's Sam, Charlotte Brooks is originally from Virginia and tells her story in the decade after Emancipation. Unlike Uncle Sam who reports "no trouble nor nothin' " (p. 10), Aunt Charlotte says "nobody knows the trouble we poor colored folks had to go through . . . !" (p. 4).

These two writers represent the two versions of slavery that were vying for popular acceptance in the literature of the late nineteenth century. Both wrote to preserve the truth about the antebellum South, but they totally disagreed about what that truth was. According to Page, the antebellum South represented a Golden Age "when men treated women chivalrously and women relied on men implicitly, when success bore no relation to wealth, and when the seventh commandment was not deemed a proper subject for conversation in mixed company" (*Novels*, Vol. 1, p. viii). According to Albert, the antebellum South was characterized by a system of slavery so corrupt that "the half was never told." Albert does not contradict Page's assertion that discussion of adultery was inappropriate in mixed company, but in her version, that silence stemmed from a conscious attempt to ignore its regular violation. Page maintained that slavery had "Christianized the negro race in a little over two centuries, impressed upon it a regard for order, and gave it the only civilization it has ever possessed since the dawn of history" (*Novels*, Vol. 12, p. 221). But Albert shows Christianity surviving despite slavery's decidedly un-Christian character. She maintains that Americans should "all thank God and rejoice that the unearthly institution has been swept away forever in a sea of blood never to rise again" (p. 161).

Thomas Nelson Page did not claim that *In Ole Virginia* was nonfiction, but he did employ devices that implied scholarly objectivity. In his dedication, he refers to the work as "this fragmentary record" of the life of his people, and prefacing the book with a note which explains that the dialect of Eastern Virginia blacks is quite different from that of other blacks, he offers a series of linguistic rules to "aid the reader." Albert's work takes a similar stance. In deference to the sexism of her time, the prefatory material to *The House of Bondage* assures scholarly objectivity by identifying its author as "Mrs. Octavia V. Rogers, deceased wife of the Rev. A. E. P. Albert, A.M., D.D." (p. v). It is both in response to social attitudes toward women writers and in reaction to Page's evocation of the Arthurian legends upon which the plantation myth was based that Albert repeatedly emphasizes the sacredness of her mission. Though the last part of *The House of Bondage* is devoted to secular achievements, Albert says, "we should not only treasure these things, but should transmit them to our children's children. That's what the Lord commanded Israel to do . . . and I verily believe that the same is his will concerning us and our bondage and deliverance in this country" (p. 130). The characters, we are assured, are "most interesting and life-like." The conversations "are not imaginary, but actual." Without referring to any specific writer, they proclaim the priority of her account by asserting that "no one can read these pages without realizing the fact that 'truth is often stranger than fiction' " (p. vi).

The House of Bondage is valuable to modern readers for both its content and its intent. It provides descriptions of life in slavery and in Reconstruction. It is the articulation of the attitudes and ideas of a significant number of American writers, and it is especially useful for understanding the philosophy of many middle-class Afro-Americans of the nineteenth century. As the prevalence of attitudes toward slavery engendered by *Uncle Tom's Cabin, In Ole Virginia, Gone with the Wind,* and even *Roots* has shown, the public has thus far continued to choose the romantic over the real. Nonetheless, concluding her book with the hymn that asks "who shall return to tell Egypt the story," Albert succeeds in planting the idea that there could be more than one version. As the work of an educated and talented black woman, *The House of Bondage* offers a somewhat less blood-stopping possibility to Alice Walker's question concerning the artistic options for our maternal ancestors. Though Albert's words themselves verify that life for black women was indeed stifling and debilitating, her work is proof that some could and did find outlets for their creative impulses.

WORKS CITED

Baym, Nina. *Woman's Fiction: A Guide to Novels by and about Women in America, 1820–1870.* Ithaca, N.Y.: Cornell University Press, 1978.

Blassingame, John W. *Slave Testimony: Two Centuries of Letters, Speeches, Interviews, and Autobiographies*. Baton Rouge, La.: Louisiana State University Press, 1977.

Brown, William Wells. *A Description of William Wells Brown's Original Panoramic Views of the Scenes in the Life of an American Slave*. London, 1850.

———. *My Southern Home; Or, the South and Its People*. 1880. New York: Negro Universities Press, 1969.

Bunyan, John. *The Pilgrim's Progress*. 1678. New York: Dodd, Mead, 1968.

Drew, Benjamin. *A North-Side View of Slavery*. Boston, 1856.

Hart, James D. *The Popular Book: A History of America's Literary Taste*. Berkeley: University of California Press, 1963.

Majors, Monroe. *Noted Negro Women: Their Triumphs and Activities*. 1893. Freeport, N.Y.: Books for Libraries Press, 1971.

Page, Thomas Nelson. *In Ole Virginia; Or, Marsh Chan and Other Stories*. 1887. New York: Scribner's, 1924.

———. *The Novels, Stories, Sketches and Poems of Thomas Nelson Page*. 12 vols. New York: Scribner's, 1908.

Penn, I. Garland. *The Afro-American Press and Its Editors*. 1891. New York: Arno, 1969.

Stowe, Harriet Beecher. *Uncle Tom's Cabin; Or, Life Among the Lowly*. 1851–52. New York: New American Library, 1981.

Walker, Alice. "In Search of Our Mothers' Gardens." *Ms.*, May 1977. Reprinted in *In Search of Our Mothers' Gardens: Womanist Prose*. San Diego: Harcourt Brace Jovanovich, 1983.

Walker, Cheryl. *The Nightingale's Burden: Women Poets and American Culture Before 1900*. Bloomington, Ind.: Indiana University Press, 1982.

Mrs. Octavia V. R. Albert.

THE HOUSE OF BONDAGE

OR

CHARLOTTE BROOKS AND OTHER SLAVES

ORIGINAL AND LIFE-LIKE, AS THEY APPEARED IN THEIR
OLD PLANTATION AND CITY SLAVE LIFE; TOGETHER
WITH PEN-PICTURES OF THE PECULIAR INSTI-
TUTION, WITH SIGHTS AND INSIGHTS
INTO THEIR NEW RELATIONS
AS FREEDMEN, FREEMEN,
AND CITIZENS

BY

MRS. OCTAVIA V. ROGERS ALBERT

WITH AN INTRODUCTION

BY

REV. BISHOP WILLARD F. MALLALIEU, D.D.

NEW YORK: HUNT & EATON
CINCINNATI: CRANSTON & STOWE
1890

Copyright, 1890, by

HUNT & EATON,

NEW YORK.

PREFACE.

THE following pages, giving the result of
conversations and other information gathered, digested, and written by Mrs. Octavia V.
Rogers, deceased wife of the Rev. A. E. P.
Albert, A.M., D.D., first appeared in the col-
umns of the *South-western Christian Advocate*,
some months after her death, as a serial story,
under the name of *The House of Bondage*.
It was received with such enthusiasm and ap-
preciation that no sooner was the story concluded than letters poured in upon the editor
from all directions, urging him to put it in
book form, so as to preserve it as a memorial
of the author, as well as for its intrinsic value as
a history of negro slavery in the Southern
States, of its overthrow, and of the mighty and
far-reaching results derived therefrom.

No special literary merit is claimed for the
work. No special effort was made in that direction; but as a panoramic exhibition of slave-
life, emancipation, and the subsequent results,
the story herein given, with all the facts
brought out, as each one speaks for himself

and in his own way, is most interesting and life-like.

The conversations herein given are not imaginary, but actual, and given as they actually occurred. No one can read these pages without realizing the fact that "truth is often stranger than fiction." As such we present it to the public as an unpretentious contribution to an epoch in American history that will more and more rivet the attention of the civilized world as the years roll around.

An only daughter unites with the writer in sending out these pages penned by a precious and devoted mother and wife, whose angelic spirit is constantly seen herein, and whose subtle and holy influence seems to continue to guide and protect both in the path over which they since have had to travel without the presence and cheer of her inspiring countenance.

To her sacred memory these pages, the result of her efforts, are affectionately inscribed.

A. E. P. ALBERT.

LAURA T. F. ALBERT.

EDITORIAL ROOMS
South-western Christian Advocate,
NEW ORLEANS, LA., *November 15, 1890.*

CONTENTS.

---◆---

CHAPTER XII.
SALLIE SMITH'S STORY.

CHAPTER XIII.
IN THE WOODS.

CHAPTER XIV.
UNCLE STEPHEN JORDON.

CHAPTER XV.
COUNTERFEIT FREE PAPERS.

CHAPTER XVI.
UNCLE CEPHAS'S STORY.

CHAPTER XVII.
A COLORED SOLDIER.

INTRODUCTION.

————⋅————

THE story of slavery never has been and never will be fully told. In the last letter that John Wesley ever wrote, addressed to Wilberforce, the great abolitionist, and dated February 24, 1791, and this only six days before his tireless hand was quieted in death, he wrote these words: " I see not how you can go through your glorious enterprise in opposing that execrable villainy " (slavery and the slave-trade), " which is the scandal of religion, of England, and of human nature. Unless God has raised you up for this very thing you will be worn out by the opposition of men and devils; but if God be for you who can be against you? Are all of them together stronger than God? O, 'be not weary in well doing.' Go on in the name of God and the power of his might till even American slavery, the vilest that ever saw the sun, shall vanish away before it."

It is because American slavery was "the vilest that ever saw the sun" that it is and will remain forever impossible to adequately portray its unspeakable horrors, its heart-breaking sorrows, its fathomless miseries of hopeless grief, its intolerable shames, and its heaven-defying and outrageous brutalities.

But while it remains true that the story can never be completely told, it is wise and well that the task should be attempted and in part performed ; and this for the reason that there are some who presume that this slavery, "the vilest that ever saw the sun," has been, and is still, of divine appointment ; in short, that from first to last it was a divine institution. It is well to remind all such people that the Almighty Ruler of the universe is not an accessory, either before or after the fact, to such crimes as were involved in slavery. Let no guilty man, let no descendant of such man, attempt to excuse the sin and shame of slave-holding on the ground of its providential character. The truth is that slavery is the product of human greed and lust and oppression, and not of God's ordering.

Then it is well to write about slavery that

the American people may know from what
depths of disgrace and infamy they rose when,
guided by the hand of God, they broke every
yoke and let the oppressed go free.   Finally,
it is well to tell, though only in part, the story
of slavery so that every man, woman, and
child of the once enslaved race may know
the exceeding mercy of God that has delivered them from the hopeless and helpless despair that might have been their portion if
the Lord God Omnipotent had not come
forth to smite in divine and righteous wrath
the proud oppressor and bring his long-suffer-
ing people out of their worse than Egyptian
bondage.

This volume, penned by a hand that now
rests in the quiet of the tomb, is a contribution
to the sum total of the story that can never be
entirely told,

In her young girlhood the author had known
the accursed system, and she knew the joy of
deliverance,   With a deep, pathetic tenderness
she loved her race ; she would gladly have
died for their enlightenment and salvation.
But she has gone to her reward, leaving behind
her the precious legacy of a sweet Christian

THE AUTHOR.

THE author of this volume, Octavia Victoria Rogers, wife of the Rev. A. E. P. Albert, D.D., was born in Oglethorpe, Macon County, Ga., of slave parentage, December 24, 1853, and was educated at Atlanta University, in that State. She and Dr. Albert first met at Montezuma, Ga., where they taught school together, in 1873; and on October 21, 1874, they were united in holy wedlock. They had an only daughter, who survives her mother. She united with the African Methodist Episcopal Church under the preaching of Bishop H. M. Turner, at Oglethorpe, Ga., and was converted and united with the Methodist Episcopal Church, under the pastorate of the Rev. Marcus Dole, at Union Chapel, New Orleans, in 1875. Her own husband baptized her at Houma, La., in 1878, during the first year of his ministry. She was an angel of mercy whose loving spirit will long be cherished by all who knew her but to love her. Now she rests from her labors, and her good works do follow her. Peace to her precious memory!

COMPILER.

THE HOUSE OF BONDAGE.

———◆———

CHAPTER I.

CHARLOTTE BROOKS.

Causes of immorality among colored people—Charlotte
Brooks—She is sold South—Sunday work.

NONE but those who resided in the South
during the time of slavery can realize the
terrible punishments that were visited upon
the slaves. Virtue and self-respect were denied
them.

Much has been written concerning the negro, and we must confess that the moral standing of the race is far from what it should be;
but who is responsible for the sadly immoral
condition of this illiterate race in the South?
I answer unhesitatingly, Their masters.

Consider that here in this Bible land, where
we have the light, where the Gospel was
preached Sunday after Sunday in all portions
of the South, and where ministers read from

the pulpit that God had made of one blood all nations of men, etc., that nevertheless, with the knowledge and teachings of the word of God, the slaves were reduced to a level with the brute. The half was never told concerning this race that was in bondage nearly two hundred and fifty years.

The great judgment-day is before us; "for we must all appear before the judgment-seat of Christ." There are millions of souls now crowned around the throne of God who have washed their robes white and are praising God, although they spent their lives in sorrow, but who will rise up in judgment and condemn this Christian nation. The Spanish Inquisition can hardly compare with the punishments visited upon this once enslaved race. But let me introduce you to some characters that will amply illustrate what I mean.

It was in the fall of 1879 that I met Charlotte Brooks. She was brought from the State of Virginia and sold in the State of Louisiana many years before the war. I have spent hours with her listening to her telling of her sad life of bondage in the cane-fields of Louisiana. She was always willing to speak of "old master and mistress." I remember one morning as she entered my home I said to her, " Good-morning, Aunt Charlotte ; how are you feeling to-day ? "

She said, " La, my child, I didn't sleep hardly last night ; my poor old bones ached me so bad I could not move my hand for a while."

" What's the cause of it ? "

" Why, old marster used to make me go out before day, in high grass and heavy dews, and I caught cold. I lost all of my health. I tell you, nobody knows the trouble I have seen. I have been sold three times. I had a little baby when my second marster sold me, and my last old marster would make me leave my child before day to go to the cane-field ; and he would not allow me to come back till ten o'clock in the morning to nurse my child. When I did go I could hear my poor child crying long before I got to it. And la, me ! my poor child would be so hungry when I'd get to it ! Sometimes I would have to walk more than a mile to get to my child, and when I did get there I would be so tired I'd fall asleep while my baby was sucking. He

2

did not allow me much time to stay with my baby when I did go to nurse it. Sometimes I would overstay my time with my baby; then I would have to run all the way back to the field. O, I tell you nobody knows the trouble we poor colored folks had to go through with here in Louisiana. I had heard people say Louisiana was a hard place for black people, and I didn't want to come; but old marster took me and sold me from my mother anyhow, and from my sisters and brothers in Virginia.

"I have never seen or heard from them since I left old Virginia. That's been more than thirty-five years ago. When I left old Virginia my mother cried for me, and when I saw my poor mother with tears in her eyes I thought I would die. O, it was a sad day for me when I was to leave my mother in old Virginia. My mother used to take her children to church every Sunday. But when I came to Louisiana I did not go to church any more. Every body was Catholic where I lived, and I had never seen that sort of religion that has people praying on beads. That was all strange to me. The older I got the more I thought of my mother's Virginia religion. Sometimes when I was away off in the cane-field at work it seemed I could hear my mother singing the 'Old Ship of Zion.' I could never hear any of the old Virginia hymns sung here, for every body was Catholic around where I stayed."

"Aunt Charlotte, did you say you *never* attended church any more after leaving Virginia?"

"No, my child; I never saw inside of a church after I came to Louisiana."

"What did you do on the Sabbath?"

"La, me! I had plenty to do. Old mistress would make me help in the kitchen on Sundays when I had nothing else to do. Mistress was Catholic, and her church was a good ways off, and she did not go often to church. In rolling season we all worked Sunday and Monday grinding cane. Old marster did not care for Sunday; he made all of us work hard on Sunday as well as any other day when he was pushed up. 'Most all the planters worked on Sunday in rolling season where I lived. In Virginia every body rested and would go to church on Sunday, and it was strange to see every body working on Sunday here. O, how I used to wish to hear some of the old Virginia hymns!

"I remember my mother used to have a minister to come to see her in Virginia, and he would read the Bible and sing. He used to sing, 'O where are the Hebrew children? Safe in the promised land.' I did not have religion when I came out here. I did not have any body to tell me any thing about repentance, but I always prayed, and the more I would pray the better I would feel. I never would fail to say my prayers, and I just thought if I could get back to my old Virginia home to hear some of my mother's old-time praises it would do my soul good. But, poor me! I could never go back to my old Virginia home."

CHAPTER II.

CHARLOTTE'S STORY.

Meeting Jane Lee from Virginia—Conversion of Charlotte
Brooks.

" FOUR years after I came to Louisiana
the speculators brought another woman
out here from my old State. She was sold to
a man near my marster's plantation. I heard
of it, and, thinks I, 'That might be some of my
kinsfolks, or somebody that knew my mother.'
So the first time I got a chance I went to see
the woman. My white folks did not want the
' niggers' to go off on Sundays; but anyhow
my old marster let me go sometimes after dinner on Sunday evenings. So I went to see
who the woman was, and I tell you, my child,
when I got in the road going I could not go
fast enough, for it just seemed to me that the
woman was one of my folks. I walked a while
and would run a while. By and by I got there.
As I went in the gate I met a man, and I asked
him what was the woman's name ; he said her

name was Jane Lee. I went around to the quarters where all the black people lived, and I found her. I went up to her and said, ' Howdy do, Aunt Jane ? ' She said, ' How do you know me, child ? ' I said, ' I heard you just came from Virginia ; I came from that State too. I just been out here four years. I am so glad to see you, Aunt Jane. Where did you come from in Virginia ? ' ' I came from Richmond. I have left all of my people in Virginia.'

"Aunt Jane was no kin to me, but I felt that she was because she came from my old home. Me and Aunt Jane talked and cried that Sunday evening till nearly dark. Aunt Jane said she left her children, and it almost killed her to ever think of them. She said one was only five years old. Her old marster got in debt, and he sold her to pay his debts. I told her I had left all of my people too, and that I was a poor lone creature to myself when I first came out from Virginia. Aunt Jane asked me did the people have churches here. I told her no ; that I had not been in a church since I came here. She had religion, and she was as good a woman as you ever saw. She

could read the Bible, and could sing so many
pretty hymns. Aunt Jane said it seemed to
her she was lost because she could not go to
church and hear preaching and singing like she
used to hear in Virginia. She said people
didn't care for Sunday in Louisiana."

"Aunt Charlotte, it must have been a joy-
ful time with you when you first saw Aunt
Jane Lee."

"Yes, I tell you. I stayed with her till evening. I was afraid old marster would not let
me go to see Aunt Jane any more, and when I
got in the road, I tell you I did not lose any
time. It was dark when I left Aunt Jane; but
before I left her house she prayed and sang,
and it made me feel glad to hear her pray and
sing. It made me think of my old Virginia
home and my mother. She sang,

"'Guide me, O thou great Jehovah,
Pilgrim through this barren land.'

"I had heard that hymn before, but had
forgot it. All next week it seemed to me I
could hear the old Virginia hymn Aunt Jane
sung for me that Sunday evening when I was
working in the cane-field.

"It was nearly rolling season when Aunt Jane first came to Louisiana, and we all was so busy working night and day I did not have a chance to see her in a long time after I left her that Sunday evening. But two or three months after that I got a chance to go to see her again. Old marster let me go and stay all day that Sunday. He said we all had made such a good year's work, and he was mighty well pleased with us. But he was not always glad and pleased with us. Sometimes he would get mad about something going wrong on the place, and he would beat every one of us and lock us up in the jail he made for us."

"What! Did he put you in jail on Sunday?"

"Yes; 'most every Sunday morning when we did not have any work to do. The next time I went to see Aunt Jane we had another happy time. She could read right good in the Bible and hymn-book, and she would read to me one or two hymns at a time. I remember she read to me about Daniel in the lions' den, and about the king having the three Hebrew children cast in the fiery furnace, and when he looked in the flames of fire he saw four men,

and one looked like the Son of God. O, how
Aunt Jane used to love to read about the Hebrew children !

"I finally got religion, and it was Aunt
Jane's praying and singing them old Virginia
hymns that helped me so much. Aunt Jane's
marster would let her come to see me sometimes, but not often. Sometimes she would
slip away from her place at night and come to
see me anyhow. She would hold prayer-
meeting in my house whenever she would come
to see me."

"Would your marster allow you to hold
prayer-meeting on his place ? "

"No, my child ; if old marster heard us
singing and praying he would come out and
make us stop. One time, I remember, we all
were having a prayer-meeting in my cabin, and
marster came up to the door and hollered out,
'*You, Charlotte*, what's all that fuss in there ? '
We all had to hush up for that night. I was
so afraid old marster would see Aunt Jane. I
knew Aunt Jane would have to suffer if her
white people knew she was off at night. Marster used to say God was tired of us all hol-
lering to him at night."

"Did any of the black people on his place believe in the teachings of their master?"

"No, my child ; none of us listened to him about singing and praying. I tell you we used to have some good times together praying and singing. He did not want us to pray, but we would have our little prayer-meeting anyhow. Sometimes when we met to hold our meetings we would put a big wash-tub full of water in the middle of the floor to catch the sound of our voices when we sung. When we all sung we would march around and shake each other's hands, and we would sing easy and low, so marster could not hear us. O, how happy I used to be in those meetings, although I was a slave ! I thank the Lord Aunt Jane Lee lived by me. She helped me to make my peace with the Lord. O, the day I was converted ! It seemed to me it was a paradise here below ! It looked like I wanted nothing any more. Jesus was so sweet to my soul ! Aunt Jane used to sing, ' Jesus ! the name that charms our fears.' That hymn just suited my case. Some-times I felt like preaching myself. It seemed I wanted to ask every body if they loved Jesus when I first got converted. I wanted to ask

old marster, but he was Creole, and did not
understand what I said much. Aunt Jane was
the cause of so many on our plantation getting
religion. We did not have any church to go
to, but she would talk to us about old Virginia,
how people done there. She said them beads
and crosses we saw every body have was nothing. She said people must give their hearts
to God, to love him and keep his command-
ments; and we believed what she said. I
never wanted them beads I saw others have,
for I just thought we would pray without any
thing, and that God only wanted the heart."

CHAPTER III.

AUNT CHARLOTTE'S FRIENDS.

Death of Aunt Charlotte's children—Jane Lee's master leaves
the neighborhood—Nellie Johnson tries to escape to her
old Virginia home.

"AUNT CHARLOTTE, what became of
your baby? were you blest to raise
it?"

"No; my poor child died when it was two
years old. Old marster's son was the father
of my child."

"Did its father help to take care of it?"

"Why, no; he never noticed my child."

"Did you have any more children?"

"Yes; but they all died."

"Why could you not rear any of them?"

"La, me, child! they died for want of attention. I used to leave them alone half of the
time. Sometimes old mistress would have
some one to mind them till they got so they
could walk, but after that they would have to
paddle for themselves. I was glad the Lord

took them, for I knowed they were better off with my blessed Jesus than with me."

Poor Charlotte Brooks! I can never forget how her eyes were filled with tears when she would speak of all her children : " Gone, and no one to care for me ! " Sometimes she failed to come and see me (for she always visited me when she was able ; never missed a day, unless she was sick, during the two years I lived near her). She was in poor health, and had no one to help her in her old age, when she really needed help. She had spent her life working hard for her masters, and after giving all of her youthful days to them was turned upon this cold, unfriendly world with nothing. She left her master's plantation with two blankets, and was several days on the road walking to get to the town of ——, and, having become so exhausted, dropped them by the way-side. She said when she arrived at her destination she had nothing but the clothes she had on her back. She was then old and feeble.

I remember she used to come and beg me to save the stale coffee for her, saying she had not eaten any thing all day. Notwithstanding

all of her poverty she was always rejoicing in
the love of God. I asked her once whether
she felt lonely in this unfriendly world.

She answered, " No, my dear; how can a
child of God feel lonesome? My heavenly
Father took care of me in slave-time. He led
me all the way along, and now he has set me
free, and I am free both in soul and body."

She said, " I heard a preacher say once
since I got free, ' Not a foot of land do I pos-
sess, not a cottage in the wilderness.' Just so
it is with me; sometimes I don't have bread
to eat; but I tell you, my soul is always feast-
ing on my dear Jesus. Nobody knows what
it is to taste of Jesus but them that has
been washed by him. Many years ago, my
white folks did not want me even to pray, and
would whip me for praying, saying it was fool-
ishness for me to pray. But the more old
marster whipped me the more I'd pray.
Sometimes he'd put me in jail; but, la, me! it
did not stop me from praying. I'd kneel
down on the jail floor and pray often, and
nearly all day Sundays. I'd fall asleep sometimes praying. Old marster would come and
call me about sundown. He would always

call out loud before he got to the jail to let
me know he was coming. I could always tell
his walk. I tell you, I used to feel rested and
good when he let me out. He let me go so
I could always be ready to go to work on
Monday morning. One Sunday night, just as
I got to my door, Aunt Jane met me. I was
just coming from the jail, too. I knowed Aunt
Jane was coming to hold prayer-meeting, and
I hurried. If old marster heard us he would
put me in jail the next Sunday morning; but,
child, that did not stop me; I was always
ready for the prayer-meeting. I told Aunt
Jane I had been in jail all day, and it was a
happy day in jail, too.

"Aunt Jane's white folks was not so hard
on her as mine was. They did not let her go
off at night, but she would slip away and come
and lead prayer-meeting at my house. She
always brought her Bible and hymn-book.
She read to us that night something like this:
'I know my Redeemer lives.'"

I said to her, "O, yes, Aunt Charlotte; I
remember it very well. It is in the book of
Job, nineteenth chapter, twenty-fifth verse."

"Well, it has been so long since I heard it

read. Wont you get the Bible and please
read it for me?"

"With much pleasure I'll read it to you.
Here it is: 'For I know that my Redeemer
liveth, and that he shall stand at the latter
day upon the earth : and though after my
skin worms destroy this body, yet in my flesh
shall I see God: whom I shall see for myself,
and mine eyes shall behold, and not another;
though my reins be consumed within me.'
I've read three verses of that chapter for you."

"Thank you, too, for it. O, how it makes
me think of them happy times in the cane-
field I used to have! I do wish I could read.
I long to read the Bible and hymn-book.
When I was in Virginia I used to study some.
I learned my A, B, C, and begun to spell some
in my blue-back spelling-book. I could spell
'ba-ker' and 'sha-dy,' and all along there in the
spelling-book; but after I came to Louisiana I
forgot every thing."

I said, "You have no hope of learning, now
that you are free, although you are at liberty
to do as you please?"

"No, my child; I can't see how to thread
my needle now. I have given all my young

days to the white folks. My eye-sight is gone.
Nothing for me to do but to wait till my Jesus
comes."

"Aunt Charlotte, what became of Jane
Lee?"

"Well, about five or six years before the
war her marster moved 'way off to Texas, and
I never saw her any more. We all cried when
she left us. We felt lost, because we had nobody to lead us in our little meetings. After
a while I begun to lead, and then some of the
others would lead. Aunt Jane caused many
of our people to get religion on our place.
Where she lived the black folks were all Catholic, and she could not do much with them.
I tell you, them Catholic people loved them
beads and crosses they used to pray to. The
last time Aunt Jane was with us she told
us her white people was going to move, and
she might never see us any more in this
world; but she said, 'Charlotte, promise me
you will meet me in heaven.' And then she
turned around to all the others in the little
cabin that night and asked them all to promise to meet her there. We all promised to
fight on till death. La, me! such crying there
3

in that little cabin that night! Aunt Jane
cried, and we cried too. It was past midnight
when we all parted. Aunt Jane had about
two miles to go after she left our place that
night. She lived about two miles from our
plantation.

"Aunt Jane said that when she came out here
a pretty woman was brought here with her by
the name of Nellie Johnson. Nellie was sold
to a mighty bad man. She tried to run away
to her old Virginia home, but the white men
caught her and brought her back. Aunt Jane
told me Nellie was almost white, and had
pretty, long, straight hair. When they got
her back they made her wear men's pants for
one year. They made her work in the field in
that way. She said they put deer-horns on
her head to punish her, with bells on them.
Aunt Jane said once while she was passing on
the levee she saw Nellie working with the
men on the Mississippi River, and she had
men's clothes on then. The white folks used
to have the levee worked on often before
the war. They were afraid the levees would
cave in."

CHAPTER IV.

CRUEL MASTERS.

Nellie Johnson is barbarously treated—Sam Wilson living
in the swamps of Louisiana—Richard's wife living on
another plantation—His master refuses to allow him to
visit her—He is caught by the patrollers and beaten
almost to death.

"AUNT JANE loved Nellie, although
Nellie was no kin to her, and she used
to talk very often to me about her white people using her so bad.   She said once that a baby
was born to Nellie on the road when she was
coming in the speculator's drove, and the speculator gave the child away to a white woman
near by where they camped that night.   The
speculator said they could not take care of the
child on the road, and told Nellie it was better
to let the white woman have the child."

"Poor Nellie !   I reckon she was trying to go
back to see her child when she was caught by
the white barbarous, creatures who evidently
were without human nature."

"Yes, I think so too," said Aunt Charlotte, "for blood is thicker than water. The white people thought in slave-time we poor darkies had no soul, and they separated us like dogs. So many poor colored people are dead from grieving at the separation of their children that was sold away from them."

"Aunt Jane said Nellie's owner was *so* bad! She said they had a man named Sam Wilson; he stayed one half of his time in the swamp. His master used to get after him to whip him, but Sam would not let his marster beat him. He would run off and stayed in the woods two and three months at a time. The white folks would set the dogs behind him, but Sam could not be caught by the dogs. The colored people said Sam greased his feet with rabbit-grease, and that kept the dogs from him. Aunt Jane said to me that she did not know what Sam used, but it looked like Sam could go off and stay as long as he wanted when the white folks got after him."

Aunt Charlotte said to me, "I tell you, my child, nobody could get me to run away in those Louisiana swamps. Death is but death, and I just thought if I'd run off in those

swamps I'd die. I used to hear old people
say it was just as well to die with fever as with
ague; and that is what I thought. Aunt Jane
said Sam was from Louisiana, and was a Catholic. She said she did not know what sort of
religion Sam's was, to let people dance and
work all day Sunday. She used to try to get
Sam to come to her prayer-meetings, but she
could not get him inside the door when they
was praying and singing. She said Sam used
to laugh at them, and call our religion ''Merican niggers' religion.' ''

"Aunt Charlotte, how many of you all used
to carry on prayer-meeting after Aunt Jane
left?''

"Well, let me count; we had Mary, Lena,
Annie, Ann, Sarah, Nancy, and Martha—seven
sisters and four brethren, Billy, Green, Jones,
and Richard. La, me! what a good time we
all used to have in my cabin on that plantation!
I think of them good, happy times we used to
have now since freedom, and wish I could see
all of them once more. I tell you, child, religion is good anywhere—at the plow-handle, at
the hoe-handle, anywhere. If you are filled
with the love of my Jesus you are happy.

Why, the best times I ever had was when I first got religion, and when old marster would put me in that old jail-house on his plantation all day Sunday.

"Richard used to be mighty faithful to his prayer-meeting, but old marster begun to be mighty mean to him. His wife lived on another plantation, and marster told Richard he had to give up that wife and take a woman on our place. Richard told old marster he did not want any other woman; he said he loved his wife and could never love any other woman. His wife was named Betty. I believe Richard would die for Betty. Sometimes Richard would slip off and go to see Betty, and marster told the patrollers every time they caught Richard on the plantation where Betty lived to beat him half to death. The patrollers had caught Richard many times, and had beat him mighty bad. So one night Richard heard the dogs coming in the woods near his wife's house, and he jumped out of his wife's window, and he went for dear life or death through the woods. He said he had to always pass over the bayou to go to his wife, but that night the patrollers were so hot behind him that he lost

his way.   He had a skiff he always went over
in, but he forgot about the skiff when they
were after him.   Richard said he just took off
every piece of clothes he had on and tied them
around his neck and swam across the bayou.
He lost his hat, and went without any all day
in the field.   Richard said when he got to the
bayou he was wet with sweat, and it was one
of the coldest nights he had ever felt in Louisiana.   He said he had about two miles to go
after he got over the bayou, and when he got
across he just slipped on his clothes he had
around his neck, and ran every step of the way
to his own plantation,   Sometimes they would
catch Richard and drive four stakes in the
ground, and they would tie his feet and hands
to each one and beat him half to death.   I tell
you, sometimes he could not work.   Marster
did not care, for he had told Richard to take
some of our women for a wife, but Richard
would not do it.   Richard loved Betty, and
he would die for her."

 " Did you say Richard was a Christian,
Aunt Charlotte ? "

 " Yes ; he used to pray and sing with us,
many, many times, all the hymns Aunt Jane

sung to us. I remember Richard used to
sing:

> " ' In the valley, in the valley,
>   There's a mighty cry to
> Jesus in the valley ;
>   So weary, so tired, Lord, I wish
> I was in heaven, hallelu.' "

Aunt Charlotte said: " Poor Richard! I
reckon he is dead now. When the Yankees
came he was one of the first ones to leave our
place, and I never heard from him any more.
I reckon if he is dead he is resting at last in
heaven. O, he had so many trials in this cold,
unfriendly world ! But he never give up praying and trusting in the Lord. Sometimes
when we all would be hoeing the cane we did
not go home to dinner, but we had our vict-
uals in a basket, and we ate under a shade-tree.
When it was hot marster used to let us have
one hour and a half at twelve o'clock. Then
we used to have good times under the shade-
trees. We used to talk of Aunt Jane Lee, and
we would sing some of her hymns till we all
would go to sleep."

CHAPTER V.

GREAT TRIBULATIONS.

The death of Lena—Her dying testimony—Aunt Charlotte's
mistress ties a servant by the thumbs—She returns and
finds her dead.

"YOU remember I told you about Lena
being one of our sisters in our prayer-
meetings," said Aunt Charlotte.

"Yes; I recollect, I believe, a great many
names you have spoken to me about every
time you came talking about your past un-
happy life; and I must confess to you that
I have enjoyed your conversation very much.
I have concluded to write the story of your
life in the cane-fields of Louisiana, and I desire
to write it in your own words, as near as possible."

"La, me, child! I never thought any body
would care enough for me to tell of my trials
and sorrows in this world! None but Jesus
knows what I have passed through."

"Tell me, Aunt Charlotte, about Lena."

"She died with small-pox, and we all grieved and missed her among us. I had to 'tend to Lena when she was sick. I was the only one that had the small-pox at that time. She told me when she first got sick she would not live. But she said, 'Charlotte, I have been working and praying for this hour. O,' she said, 'God has promised to lead all who will follow him. I have been toiling so long; now I'm about to cross over.' I said to Lena, 'Yes, my sister, Jesus stopped dying to redeem one soul on the cross. Remember how Aunt Jane used to read to us that Jesus promised the thief on the cross that he should be with him in paradise.' Lena asked me to sing, 'On Jordan's stormy banks I stand, and cast a wistful eye.' O, I can never forget Lena! She is in heaven this day, I believe. We learned that hymn from Aunt Jane Lee. Just before Lena died she said, 'Glory be to God and the Lamb forever! Safe at last, safe at last!' These were her last words to me. I remember when old marster got mad with Lena he used to put her in jail all day on Sunday and give her nothing but bread and water to eat."

"Aunt Charlotte, my heart throbs with sym-

years old. Ella's mother did not live with her.
Mistress had no more feeling for her than she
had for a cat. She used to beat her and pull
her ears till they were sore. She would crack
her on the head with a key or any thing she
could get her hands on till blood would ooze
out of the poor child's head. Mistress's mother
give Ella to her, and when Ella got to be
about eighteen mistress got jealous of her
and old marster. She used to punish Ella all
sorts of ways. Sometimes she tied her up by
her thumbs. She could do nothing to please
mistress. She had been in the habit of tying
Ella up, but one day she tied her up and left
her, and when she went back she found Ella
dead. She told old marster she did not intend
to kill her, that she only wanted to punish her.
Mistress and marster did not live good after
she killed Ella, for a long time. Poor Ella! I
don't know where she is to-day. She was a
Catholic. You could always see her with her
beads and cross in her pocket. She is in purgatory, I reckon; for the Catholics say the
priest can hold mass and get any body out for
so much money. But nobody held mass for
Ella, and so she will have to stay in purgatory.

But, I tell you, I believe there is only two places for us—heaven and torment. If we miss heaven we must be forever lost.”

“Yes, Aunt Charlotte, that's the teaching of the Bible.”

“Aunt Jane used to tell us, too, that the children of Israel was in Egypt in bondage, and that God delivered them out of Egypt; and she said he would deliver us. We all used to sing a hymn like this:

“‘My God delivered Daniel, Daniel, Daniel;
My God delivered Daniel,
    And why not deliver me too ?
He delivered Daniel from the lions' den,
Jonah from the belly of the whale,
The three Hebrew children from the fiery furnace,
    And why not deliver me too ?’

“O, you ought to hear Richard sing that hymn! I never can forget Aunt Jane, for when old marster used to be so hard on me it seemed I'd have to give up sometimes and die. But then the Spirit of God would come to me and fill my heart with joy. It seemed the more trials I had the more I could pray.”

“Aunt Charlotte, you remind me of Pilgrim's Progress.”

“Yes, I remember about Pilgrim traveling

from the City of Destruction to the Celestial City."

I said, " His name was John Bunyan. He was confined in jail twelve years on account of his religion."

" Was he a slave too ? "

" No ; he was not a slave, but at the time he lived people were persecuted on account of their religious belief."

" Yes, my child, that's the way it is here in Louisiana. The most of the white people were Catholics around where I lived, and we poor darkies that did not believe in Catholic relig-ion had to suffer on account of it. But that's the time a true child of God prays, when he gets in trouble. For I know the most peace-ful hours were when marster would put me in jail all day Sunday. We used to sing this song :

> " ' O, brother, where was you ?
> O, brother, where was you ?
> O, brother, where was you
> When the Lord come passing by?
>> Jesus been here,
>> O, he's been here;
>> He's been here
>> Soon in the morning;
>> Jesus been here,
>> And blest my soul and gone.'

"Yes, my dear child, that hymn filled me with joy many a time when I'd be in prison on Sunday. I'd sit all day singing and praying. I tell you, Jesus did come and bless me in there. I was sorry for marster. I wanted to tell him sometimes about how sweet Jesus was to my soul; but he did not care for nothing in this world but getting rich. He had a brother living in Georgia. I believe he did not believe in Catholic religion.

"We all knowed his brother from Georgia, because he used to always come out in rolling season to see us make sugar. He used to love to hear us sing. Once while he was out he took mighty sick, and I had to attend to him. He asked me to pray for him. I said, 'Yes, sir; I will pray for you, but you must touch the hem of the Saviour's garment yourself.' 'Yes,' he said, 'I am a Christian, and have been for many years.' We used to hear him sing, when he was riding over the field looking at the cane, one hymn he used to like. It was this:

> " ' When my heart first believed,
>   What a joy I received,
> What a heaven in Jesus's name !'

" I knowed that hymn, and it used to do me good to hear him sing Aunt Jane's hymns. He married a woman in Georgia; and he had lived there so long till he almost forgot how to speak French. Old marster did not like 'Merican people. Old mistress used to have balls on Sunday. She had me and her cook fixing all day Sunday for the ball on Sunday night sometimes. Mistress's religion did not make her happy like my religion did. I was a poor slave, and every body knowed I had relig- ion, for it was Jesus with me every-where I went. I could never hear her talk about that heavenly journey."

CHAPTER VI.

A KIND MISTRESS.

Death of Aunt Charlotte's mistress—Second marriage of
   Aunt Charlotte's master—George, one of Aunt Charlotte's fellow-servants, beaten nearly to death and one
   eye put out for being overheard talking about freedom.

"MY mistress took sick with fever, and we
all did not think she was bad off. We
knowed she had been used to being sick now
and then, but would soon be up. But she
never left her bed alive. They sent for the
priest just before she died. He greased her
with something, I believe, and they say she
took the sacrament from the priest that day.
But I am afraid she is lost. She died just like
she lived. Mistress did not live right, and she
did not die right. The old saying, ' Just as the
tree falls, just so it lies.' So many times
I used to want to talk to her about her religion ;
but she seemed to know every thing, and I was
a poor creature that knowed nothing but how
to work for marster in the cane-field. Marster

4

had mass for mistress, I don't know how many times; but what good did it do her soul?"

"None whatever, Aunt Charlotte; we must make our peace with God before we leave the world. This world is our dressing-room, and if we are not dressed up and prepared to meet God when we die we can never enter the promised land; for there is no preparation beyond the grave. The Bible tells us, 'Whatsoever a man soweth, that shall he also reap.'"

"Yes," said Aunt Charlotte; "I have heard Aunt Jane say she used to hear the preacher in Virginia preach that very text. She used to say, 'The wages of sin is death; but the gift of God is eternal life.'"

"Why, Aunt Charlotte, she was equal to a preacher; she was certainly above the average of colored women."

"Yes, my child, she was raised in Virginia, and she learned how to read before she came out here."

"Aunt Charlotte, at the death of your mistress did you all get on any better with your master?"

"No, my child; old marster always ruled that place. He went to Georgia and married a lady,

and we all was mighty glad he married a 'Merican woman, because we thought we would be
allowed to go to church. But; la, my child! she
did not believe in Catholic religion, but old
marster ruled her and she could not do what
she wanted. It would do your soul good to
hear her sing the hymns when she came to our
place. Sometimes on Sunday mornings she
would go out in the flower-garden, and we
would hear her singing,

"' Happy day, happy day,
When Jesus washed my sins away.'

"They did not live good together. I always
believed he was sorry he married her, for she was
not Catholic. I used to see her crying when
he would leave her and go off. He was rich,
but that did not make his last wife happy.
She was a pretty young woman, but she soon
began to look old after she came to our place.
She would let us have our little meetings, but
he would not allow her to have any thing to do
with us. I liked old marster's last wife. She
used to come in the kitchen on Sundays and
talk about religion. She wanted to go to
'Merican church, but it was so far away she

could not go often. It was about twenty miles
away from our place. Sometimes, though, she
went. I remember she told me that the minister took for his text one Sunday morning,
'Rest for the people of God.' I said to mistress, 'La! how I wish I could heard that
preached ! ' She said to me, 'Yes, Charlotte, it
would do your soul good to hear that minister
preach.' I knowed mistress could not let me
go to church. Marster didn't like 'Merican or
Protestant religion, and he didn't want none of
us to go. I just tell you, my child, Catholic
religion and 'Merican religion can't go together.
A woman does mighty bad business marrying
a Catholic man if she believes in 'Merican religion. They don't live peaceful together. We
never had any more dancing on Sunday nor
Monday after marster married that 'Merican
woman. Sometimes marster's kinfolks would
come to see his last wife on Sunday evening,
but they did not have any pleasure together.
You know oil and water wont mix, and just so
with the Catholic and 'Merican religions. They
believe our religion is nothing."

"If the Catholics could feel that spark of
heavenly love that pervades the soul of every

true converted child of God, Aunt Charlotte,
they would never doubt the American religion."

"I believe so, my child. When the Yankees
came I left the plantation, and I don't know
what become of mistress after I left her; but I
think of her now, and would be so glad to see
her. If she is dead I believe she is at rest, for
she used to talk about that Christian journey
so much."

"Yes, Aunt Charlotte, I knew of white
women who were truly converted here in the
South, and who took pleasure in teaching the
colored people the Scriptures. I knew, in the
State of Georgia, white families who would
compel their slaves to attend church on Sundays and would not allow them to work on that
day. If they did not attend church they would
go out in the colored people's cabins and read
the Bible to them very often on Sundays and
explain it to them. I don't mean to say that
the whites did this as a general thing, but
many of them did."

"But how could they have good religion and
keep us poor darkies in bondage and beat us
half to death?"

"Well, Aunt Charlotte, I am hardly able to answer you satisfactorily, I must confess, for when I pause and think over the hard punishments of the slaves by the whites, many of whom professed to be Christians, I am filled with amazement. Religion fills our souls with love for God and humanity. The Bible, moreover, says, 'We know we have passed from death unto life, because we love the brethren.' And you know as a rule there were comparatively few colored people during the period of slavery, or even now, but what are members of some Christian denomination. So they were their brethren through Christ.

"Aunt Charlotte, did you slaves know what brought on this last war?"

"Yes, child; we heard people say the Yankees was fighting to free us. But, my child, it was death for us poor darkies to talk about freedom. We had a man on our place named George. Marster did not like him much, no how, and one day he overheard George talking about freedom; and, I tell you, he half killed him that day. He beat George a while, and then would make the driver beat him a while. They say they give George nine hundred lashes

and then made him wash all over in salt water.
While he was whipping him he put out one of
George's eyes. Poor George didn't have but
one eye after that. But, let me tell you, it was
not three months after that before marster
bought a fine horse, and he used to drive him
to his buggy all the time. Old marster loved
that horse better than he loved his wife, I
think. One morning he was driving out, and
the horse got scared at something and run
away, broke the buggy all to pieces, throwed
marster flat on the ground, and broke his leg.
Old marster never did walk without a crutch
after that. I tell you I was sorry for marster,
for he suffered so much when he was down in
the bed from his broken leg. But I thought
no good would ever come of him when he put
out George's eye."

"Yes," said I, "we read in the Bible that
'fools, because of their transgression, and because of their iniquities, are afflicted.'"

CHAPTER VII.

BROKEN-DOWN FREEDMEN.

Aunt Charlotte splitting rails—In Sunday-school—Joe Sims, a
runaway, sleeping in the woods with rattlesnakes—Eating out of trash-boxes.

"AUNT CHARLOTTE, people who never
knew any thing about slave-life in the
South can hardly credit the reports that have
been circulated by those who have resided
here. For it seems to me that the terrible
treatment the slaves received from the hands
of their masters was more than any human
being could bear."

"But, my child, every word is true. I can't
tell you half what my two eyes have seen since
I have been in Louisiana. The white folks did
not take the niggers for nothing more than
brutes. They would take more time with fine
horses, and put them up to rest. We poor
darkies were never allowed to rest. I have
split rails many and many a day, and sometimes my back would almost break when I'd

have to roll logs, but I had to keep pulling
along. When night came I could hardly drag
one foot before the other. I'd go to my bed,
and it would be wet where it leaked through
the top of the house, and I'd just fall in it and
would not know it was wet with water till next
morning. I'd find leeches sticking to my legs,
and blood would be all on my feet. I'd get
them in the woods cutting wood. I tell you,
if you get a leech on you it will draw like a
blister. When I came to my house at night I
was too tired to eat. I went to bed a many
time hungry—was too broke down to cook my
supper after working all the day hard."

"Why, I can't see what kept you alive, Aunt
Charlotte, till now!"

"The dear Lord and Saviour kept me alive,
and he is still taking care of me. Ever since
I came to town I never miss going to church;
and the other Sunday morning I went into
the Sunday-school before church began, and I
heard the children sing something like this:

"'All the way my Saviour leads me.'

And when them children sang that it filled
my eyes with tears, for I just thought how

good the Lord had been to me. He had brought me through so much hardship, and I said, ' Here I am, Lord, blest to sit down and hear singing and preaching.' It was the first time I had ever heard that hymn, and I thought it was so sweet to my soul."

"Yes," I said, "it's one of my favorite hymns." " Wont you get your book and read it for me if you please? " " Here it is:

> " ' All the way my Saviour leads me;
>   What have I to ask beside ?
> Can I doubt his tender mercy,
>   Who through life has been my guide ?
> Heavenly peace, divinest comfort,
>   Here by faith in him I dwell !
> For I know whate'er befall me,
>   Jesus doeth all things well.

> " ' All the way my Saviour leads me;
>   Cheers each winding path I tread ;
> Gives me grace for every trial ;
>   Feeds me with the living bread ;
> Though my weary steps may falter,
>   And my soul athirst may be,
> Gushing from the Rock before me,
>   Lo ! a spring of joy I see.

> " ' All the way my Saviour leads me;
>   O, the fullness of his love !
> Perfect rest to me is promised
>   In my Father's house above ;

When my spirit, clothed immortal,
  Wings its flight to realms of day,
This my song through endless ages—
  Jesus led me all the way.' "

"O, bless the Lord for the chance of hearing those words! They suit my case. I want to sing that very hymn in glory. Yes, 'Jesus led me all the way.' Sometimes I don't know where I'll get a piece of bread when I get up in the morning, but still I'm living and praising God. We poor old colored people were turned off the plantations without any thing in this world to go on—turned out like sheep iñ the woods. Mrs. B——promised me last week if I'd come around and wash dishes for her every day she would give me the scraps she had left always at meals. I thank the Lord for that much. I don't need much in this world, no how—just enough to keep soul and body together. I know I can't stay here much longer, I don't want nothing in this world. If I can just get a little coffee every morning and a piece of bread I am satisfied."

"Aunt Charlotte, you can't always get a little coffee and bread?"

"No, child."

"Why, it seems you could get enough to do

among the different families here in this town."

" No, bless your soul; the most of the white people don't want me—they say I am too old. I can't see how to work, and what I could do they wont let me."

"Aunt Charlotte, I see a great many old, feeble-looking men and women around in this place."

"Yes, many of them just like me—nobody to help them, and they are too old to do work, and just go wandering about picking up any thing they can get. Poor old Brother Joe Sims picks up, one half of his time, scraps out of the trash-boxes. He picks up rags for a living, and I have seen him eating out of the box of trash sometimes. Brother Joe is a member of our church; he never misses to come to church on Sundays. He came from Virginia too. He used to tell me how he stayed in the woods after he was sold out here. He said once his marster got after him to whip him and he would not let him do it. He said he run away in the woods for a long time. Brother Joe said he had a bed made of moss and limbs of trees in the woods. He said

every day he would go off and get something
to eat wherever he could, and then go back to
his moss bed at night. You ought to hear
him tell about the rattlesnakes that used to
keep him company in the woods. He said the
snakes got so used to him that they stayed
under his moss bed at night. Sometimes he
could hear them turning over under him.
The snakes would go off in the day and come
back at night. He could kill them if he
wanted to, but he was glad to have them for
company.

"You see, my child, God will take care of
his people," said Aunt Charlotte. " He will
hear us when we cry. True, we can't get any
thing to eat sometimes, but trials make us pray
more. I just tell you, I don't sleep all night
no night. I can't; for the Spirit of God wakes
me up between midnight and day, and I just
gets right down on my knees and tells my
Father all about my trials here below. We
all are free, but we can't stop praying; we
must keep on; we aint out of Egypt yet.
We have been let loose, and now we are just
marching on to a better land."

"Aunt Charlotte, it really makes me feel

happy to hear you express your faith in the
goodness of God. He has wrought wonderful
works for the colored people here. He has
raised up friends all through the North for
them. Never was education so cheap as now.
School-houses are being built all through the
South for them. The money is being given
by philanthropic Christians to educate the
colored children. Education and morality will
lift the colored people up out of the degrada-
tion in which they have been kept so long by
their educated white Christian brethren."

"But, my child, so few of the children can
go to school about here. We have school six
months in this town, and you can see the children coming for a little while, and then they
have to leave to go to work in the cane-field.
All are poor, and they have to work to get
something to eat. The children learn to read
a little, and after that they leave school. I
know a few go off to New Orleans sometimes
to school, but only two or three. O, I wish
the good times had come when I was young!"

CHAPTER VIII.

THE CURSE OF WHISKY.

The Methodist Episcopal Church—The colored people and
whisky-drinking—When the Yankees came to Louisiana
—The end of Aunt Charlotte's story.

"AUNT CHARLOTTE, which church are
you a member of here?"

"I am a member of the Methodist Church.
Our minister said the other Sunday the Methodist Church divided on account of slavery
many years ago, and that the old mother-
Church never failed to crush out slavery at
every turn. It seems to me every Christian
that honors God in the pardoning of their sins
ought to agree to every thing that is holy and
good. How could any Christian man believe
it was right to sell and buy us poor colored
people just like we was sheep? I tell you, I
have seen black people, in slave-time, drove
along—may be one hundred in a drove—just
like hogs to be sold. Sometimes men were
sold from their wives and mothers from their

children. I saw a white man in Virginia sell his own child he had by a colored woman there. They say a 'Merican man never would take care of his children he would have in slave-time by the black women, as a Frenchman would here in Louisiana. Old marster used to say niggers did not have a soul, and I reckon all the white folks thought so too."

"Aunt Charlotte, education and religion taught them better."

"Yes, child; for when I first got religion I did not want to hurt an ant. Every thing was love, joy, and peace with me. I sometimes think my people don't pray like they used to in slavery. You know when any child of God gets trouble that's the time to try their faith. Since freedom it seems my people don't trust in the Lord as they used to. 'Sin is growing bold, and religion is growing cold.' That's what our minister says sometimes."

"Aunt Charlotte, I am told that the colored people are suffering more from the habit of indulging in strong drink than any thing else here in the South."

"Yes, my dear child; in the time of slavery

one hardly knew what whisky was in some places ; but since freedom we see men and women drunk.   About a year ago I went out to a plantation near this town and I saw two hundred liquor-barrels emptied and laying around on the place.   All the planters keep whisky for the laborers, and they spend more money for drink than they do for any thing else.   They don't get much for their work, no way, and I can't see how the hired men can drink so much whisky.''

" Aunt Charlotte, how much are the men paid per day? ''

" They get only fifty and sixty cents a day. Some of the men have a wife and four or five children to take care of.   They have their wife to help them, but, la, me ! the wife's help is next to nothing in the field.   The women can't get as much as the men, no way, although they go out and work hard all day long and keep up with the men too.''

" I can't see, Aunt Charlotte, how any man who has four or five children can afford to drink when he makes only fifty and sixty cents per day ! ''

" Well, I tell you how they do.   They al-
5

ways have an account open in the plantation
store, and they allow them to get any thing
they want from the store. If they come out
in debt at the end of the year they work on
the next year and pay it. Sometimes they find
at the end of the year they owe the planter
fifty dollars for whisky. Why, my dear child,
I know children on some of them plantations
ten years old never had a pair of shoes to keep
their feet off the cold, frosty ground since they
were born."

"Yes, I am induced to believe, Aunt Charlotte, that whisky is causing more suffering
among the colored people than slavery, or as
much, any way. The temperance society that
has been lately organized in this town is destined to do much good among the colored
people."

"Yes ; the preacher holds temperance meeting every Sunday evening now in our church
after preaching. It would do your heart good
to hear our sisters make little temperance
speeches after preaching on Sunday evenings.
We had a sister named Ellen, and her husband
was named Jack. Sister Ellen couldn't read,
but she would make her speech whenever her

time came around on Sunday evening. She
said, ' Brothers and sisters, I don't know much
and can't say much, but let me tell you all,
since Jack got in this little society the preacher
started here he is changed all over. Why,
Jack used to sleep in the gutters of water
one half of his time at night. I used to
have to pick Jack up almost every night and
carry him home. He's got religion too. Jack
is a good man. He did not care any thing for
his children, and I could not get a cup of coffee one half of my time when he drank gin ;
but now I get coffee, sugar, and shoes, and he
takes care of his children too. Now,' she said,
' come up, all you men sitting over yonder,
come and join this little society.' We all
would laugh at Sister Ellen, for she seemed so
earnest in her talk. She would shake her fist
and knock on the railing around the altar
whenever she got up to speak. She did not
mind us laughing, though ; she went right on.
One time after she got through speaking
about ten men and women came up and joined
the ' little society.' "

"Aunt Charlotte, it is a great pity, and, indeed, a great sin, for the planters to keep

whisky on their plantations for their laborers. It's a temptation set before them."

"Yes; I always thought so too; but the planters don't care just so they get them to do the work good. They don't get too drunk to work through the week; but on Sundays they lay about almost dead drunk on some plantations. I tell you, I am afraid whisky will ruin my people yet."

"I trust not, Aunt Charlotte. There is a great temperance movement going on throughout this country, and we are destined to see good results from it. We hope to have a law to prevent the sale of any intoxicating drinks. It may be many years, but I believe we shall have it."

"I trust in the Lord to bring it to pass. Our people suffer more than any body, for we were turned loose without any thing, and we got no time to waste. We must get education, and, above all things in this world, get religion, and then we will be ladies and gentlemen."

"Yes; I believe religion and education will lift them upon a level with any other of the civilized races on earth. It's true we see so

much prejudice manifested almost every-where
we go ; but we must wait on the Lord. He has
promised to carry us through."

Aunt Charlotte said : " It makes me so glad
to see my people going to school. Never did
I think to see these good times ! White people would not let us learn the book in slave-
time. I used to want to learn when I was
young, but they would not even let us have a
book to study in. La, child ! when the Yankees came out here our eyes began to open,
and we have been climbing ever since, Whenever I see a Yankee it makes me mighty glad,
for I just feel that God sent them down here
to set us free. When the war was going on I
heard they was fighting for us. I tell you,
when it was going on I did not cease to pray.
We done the praying and the Yankees done
the fighting, and God heard our prayers 'way
down here in these cane-fields. Many times I
have bowed down between the cane-rows, when
the cane was high, so nobody could see me,
and would pray in the time of the war ! I used
to say, ' O, my blessed Lord, be pleased to
hear my cry ; set me free, O my Lord, and I
will serve you the balance of my days.' I

knowed God had promised to hear his children when they cry, and he heard us way down
here in Egypt."

Thus ends the story of Aunt Charlotte's life
in the cane-fields of Louisiana. But the half
cannot be told.

turn a listening ear to the sad cry of these
needy souls whom Christ died to save.

> " Whatsoever thing thou doest
> To the least of mine and lowest,
> That thou doest unto me."

It is, indeed, a mystery to those who have
witnessed the cruelty of the whites in the
South toward the poor, ignorant, innocent, de-
graded, and helpless people whom God, in his
own good time, has liberated.   Here, with an
open Bible, a Christian land of prosperity for
the Caucasian ; but, alas ! what for the negro?
O, bishops and ministers of every Christian
denomination in this Southland, how can you,
as heralds of Jesus, sit quietly by and see the
needs of seven millions or more of human
souls crying in the valley of sin and sorrow and
not give a listening ear to them?   Go out into
the highways and hedges and tell them of
Jesus, mighty to save.   Do you preach that
Jesus tasted death for *every man?*   How
strange that here in the South the Methodist
Church and the Baptist Church seem ready
and willing to send missionaries to other coun-
tries, and are not willing to extend a helping
hand to these needy souls who have served

them so long and faithfully! Behold your
" brethren in black " at your doors; arise and
let them in. And the least you do for Jesus
will be precious in his sight.

During my stay in the town of ——, where
I met Charlotte Brooks, I met another slave
who had formerly lived in the State of Georgia.
He was a cooper by trade, and had a wife and
three children. John Goodwin was his name.
Here in the South it is considered by the black
people a mark of respect to address the oldeɪ
men and women as " uncle " and "aunt;" and,
as Mr. Goodwin was aged and gray, I, too, soon
learned to address him as " Uncle John." So
one day, as he passed by, I called to him and
said :

" Uncle John, Aunt Charlotte tells me that
you formerly lived in the State of Georgia. I
came from there when I was young, and am
therefore very glad to meet you. Wont you
come around to see me some time and have a
good talk about our native home? "

He said : " Yes, ma'am; I'd be mighty glad
to come 'round and have a good long talk
about my old home. It makes me glad to see
any body from Georgia. I came out here to

Louisiana long before the war begun. When my old marster died all his property was divided among his children, and my marster's oldest daughter drawed me, and she married and moved here to Louisiana."

Uncle John then bowed his head and said, "Good-morning, ma'am."

He promised that he would come in a few days and bring his wife, Lorendo, with him. Sure enough, in a few days in comes Uncle John and his wife. As he entered he said :

"Here's my wife, Mrs. A. She is a Creole woman ; her name is Lorendo. I left my other wife in Georgia when the white folks brought me out here."

What a great pity that husbands and wives should thus have been separated !

"That's the cry all over the South, Uncle John," I said.

"Yes, ma'am; I thought when I left wife and children in Georgia it would break my heart; but, bless the Lord, I'm still on pleading terms of mercy."

I said, " Did you find by moving to this State you fared any better?"

"No, ma'am ; the white folks were bad

every-where. The only difference I found out
here is the white people did not regard the
Sabbath day. Why, ma'am, they would make
the darkies work all day Sunday sometimes
when they was pushed up with the grass in
the cane."

"Yes, I've learned they desecrated the Sabbath to a fearful extent; and even now, Uncle
John, we see almost every body selling and
buying on Sunday. I presume it is a habit
that they have indulged so long that they
hardly know how to discontinue it. Even
among the Protestant churches we find many
who disregard the Sabbath in this State."

Aunt Lorendo said: "Why, ma'am, I never
knowed nothing else but buying and selling all
my life on Sunday. I was born right here in
Louisiana, and the priest and every body else
always got whatever they wanted on Sunday.
I did not know it was wrong."

I asked Uncle John if he knew Aunt Charlotte Brooks.

He said: "Yes, ma'am; I been knowing Sister Charlotte for a long time. She is a good
member of our church here. She suffers with
rheumatism mighty bad."

"Yes, Uncle John; I've learned to love her since my stay here. She has spent many hours with me telling of her slave-life in this State. I don't think there are many women who have gone through the hardship that she has and endured it. She must have had an extraordinary constitution."

"Why, ma'am, Sister Charlotte just suffered like the most of us did. Sometimes you could find white people who treated we poor slaves right good; but it was not often. Why, in my young days I used to pick cotton all day and half of the night. My marster used to set a tree on fire for us to see how to pick cotton. I have picked as much as three and four hundred pounds of cotton in one day a many a time. I tell you, my old marster used to work us half to death trying to get rich."

In many portions of the State of Georgia there are high and rugged hills. Here we find low and marshy land, and it is therefore very unhealthy for weak and feeble persons, especially those who suffer with any throat or lung troubles. Uncle John related many thrilling accounts of his slave-life in the State of Georgia. He had a baby brother named Jim, and his mother, having to work in the field every day, was compelled to leave her children. It was a very common habit, in some portions of the State, to build the cabins upon the high hills with earth floors; and Uncle John's mother always left the baby in the cradle, during the day, all alone. So one day she was in the field plowing, and a heavy rain-storm came up, and she hastened to her cabin as soon as she could; for she knew her dear little babe was there, only two years of age, and no one with it, and it poured down through the cabin, and also washed through it, like a branch of water.

Uncle John said: "I tell you, when my mammy got to her cabin she saw where little Jim had been in the cradle; but he was out and gone, she did not know where. Mammy saw where the rain had washed clear through her house, and she said she knowed the branch was not far from the house, and big gutters all the way between her house and the creek; so she went down toward the creek as fast as she could, and there she found little Jim being rolled over and over by the rain. Mammy said Jim was almost to the creek when she took him up. My mammy cried a while and she prayed a while when she found her child that day."

Uncle John declared that the little baby boy who was picked up almost one fourth of a mile from her cabin that stormy day is now living in the State of Alabama. He is a local preacher there.

" My mammy had to work hard all day long with all the balance of the men. She was a mighty smart woman," said Uncle John. " After working all day in the cotton-field she would come home and work half of the night for herself and children. She used to wash, patch, spin, and cook for the next day to carry out in the field."

CHAPTER X.

A CONVERTED CATHOLIC.

Going to church on Sunday in Georgia—Ill-treatment of
Uncle John's daughter—Aunt Lorendo's second visit—
Her conversion from Romanism—Her Cousin Albert to
be hung—Hattie runs away to the woods and gives birth
to a child there.

I ASKED Uncle John if he did not find it
hard, after moving to Louisiana, that he
could not attend church as he used to in Georgia.

"Yes, madam; I missed the good preaching
I used to hear in Georgia. We all walked a
many a time ten and twelve miles to go to
church there on Sunday. My mammy used to
cook on Saturday for us all to carry with us on
Sunday; and we all would get up before day
on Sunday morning and start off to church.
I tell you, we would walk a while and rest
a while under the shade of the trees on the
road-side. Sometimes we would get to the
church before ten o'clock. They always

begun preaching at eleven o'clock, and we'd be afraid we would not get there in time. My wife in Georgia was named Nancy; she got religion while the minister was preaching. I had religion before my wife did. Nancy had been praying for a long time. She used to go away off in the woods to pray. I went in the woods many times to pray; I thought I could pray better in the swamp."

Uncle John said: "I remember until this day the text that minister took that Sunday when Nancy got religion. It was, 'Behold, I stand at the door and knock.' I tell you, ma'am, Nancy shouted, and was so happy we could hardly get her home that evening. She shouted all along the road as we walked. We all got happy on our way back that night, and I do believe it was ten o'clock before we reached home. Nancy cried out in church when she was converted, and said, 'Glory be to God and the Lamb forever! I am washed clean by the blood of Jesus.'"

Uncle John said: "Poor Nancy! I reckon she is dead now. She was our white folks' cook. We had a little girl ten years old; she waited in the house. They would blindfold her and beat my poor child half to death. I tell you, my heart would bleed sometimes when I'd see how my child was treated. I could do nothing for my wife and children. I was not allowed to open my mouth."

Uncle John could hardly suppress the tears from his eyes while relating the sad condition of his wife and the inhuman abuse of his daughter when he left them in Georgia, although it had been many years. He said, "O, if I could only see my children once more!"

He left me that evening with the promise that he would come to see me again, and that he would have his wife visit me too. Aunt Lorendo said, "I know where you live now, and will stop to see you sometimes when I pass." I told her I thanked her, and that I should be pleased to have her stop at any time. I said, "It affords me real pleasure to have yourself and husband relate your trials and sorrows that you both had to endure so long."

It was not long before Aunt Lorendo called again. As she entered the door I said: "Good morning, Aunt Lorendo; how are you feeling?"

"I am pretty well," she said.

I asked, "How is Uncle John?"

6

"O, he is well as might be expected for an old man. You know he passed through so much hardship in slavery, he will never feel well till he gets home. He caught so much cold and is so painful he can't hardly rest at night. But," she added, " I trust we both will rest by and by."

"Yes, Aunt Lorendo, the Bible promises that there is ' rest for the people of God.' And it affords us joy to know that although we have trials and tribulations here we who prove faithful till death shall enter that ' rest prepared for the people of God.' "

" Yes, ma'am ; I used to be Catholic, but I never knowed how good the 'Merican religion was till I married John. He was a member of the 'Merican church, and he got me to go with him on Sundays to his church ; and the more I went the more I liked it. I made my first communion when I was fifteen years old in the Catholic Church, and I was a Catholic for a long time. I tell you, I used to think no other religion was good like mine. I made fun of the 'Merican religion ; but now, ever since I been changed, I feel like I been new born. I tell you that 'Merican religion makes any body feel happy all over; it runs all through you, down from your head to the very soles of your feet! But Catholic religion is all doings and no feeling in the heart."

"Aunt Lorendo, when you were a Catholic did you always confess every thing to the priest ? "

"Yes, ma'am ; I'd tell the priest every thing I did wicked. But, I tell you, one time I had a cousin that told the priest he wanted to get free, and asked him to pray to God to set him free, and, bless your soul, ma'am, the priest was about to have my cousin hung. The priest told my cousin's marster about it, and they was talking strong about hanging my cousin. They had my cousin up and made him tell who had told him any thing about freedom. But the priest managed some way to save my poor cousin. Madam, I tell you, from that day on I could not follow my Catholic religion like I had. You know the Catholics always tell the priest every thing; they talk to him like a father ; and so it was with my cousin. He would tell the priest every thing. He never thought he would tell on him."

"Why, Aunt Lorendo, don't you know the

Catholics were bitterly opposed to the emancipation of the slaves? Why, the pope was
the only power in the world that recognized
the Confederacy. They assisted powerfully in
carrying on the civil war. It is strange, however, that we find that here in the South
among the Catholic churches we don't see the
caste prejudice so clearly manifested among
all the other denominations; nevertheless,
they believe God has made the black man to
serve the white man.

"Aunt Lorendo, Aunt Charlotte has spent
many hours with me telling of her slave-life
here in Louisiana, and as you were born and
reared here perhaps the revelation of your experiences will be as thrilling as hers. I must
say that she has caused tears to flow from my
eyes many a day while relating her hardships."

"Yes," replied Aunt Lorendo; "we come
through so much hardship sometimes I wonder why we poor darkies did not all die out
in slave-time. They used to run away in the
woods and stay till all the clothes was off their
backs. Why, ma'am, I know one time, right
in my neighborhood, one woman—her mistress
always had the overseer beating her — her

name was Hattie—she used to run away and
live in the woods for three and four weeks at
a time. I remember I was out in the field
hoeing cane in slave-time, and as I was getting
toward the end of my row of cane I heard
somebody over the fence in the woods calling
me, and at first I did not know what to do ;
but as I looked up through the fence I saw it
was Hattie. Madam, if you believe me, Hattie was almost naked that day ! She asked me
to give her something to eat; and I did give
her all I had in my bucket. Hattie said, ' Lorendo, I had my child here in the woods ; it is
dead and I buried it in a piece of my frock-
shirt.' I said, 'La ! Hattie, how in the world
did you do by yourself ?' She said, ' I don't
know, Lorendo. All I can tell, God took care
of me in these woods. O,' she said, ' I have
so many trials with my mistress. I try to satisfy her, but nothing I do pleases her. I left
my home, I reckon, two months. I tore all my
clothes off of me. See ! I am almost naked.'
I said, ' Hattie, why did you run away ?'
' Because, Lorendo,' she said, ' old mistress
came up to me one morning and went to beating me with a big iron key all over my head,

Hattie! I heard when they got her home her
marster put her in stocks every night and
would beat her every morning. Hattie at last
died from punishment, I believe."

Now, my readers, these are not imaginary
thoughts, but they were actually related to me.
While I pen these lines I can hardly suppress
the tears when I picture to my mind a poor
woman marching before six men, six horses,
and ten blood-hounds with blood oozing from
her feet. There were none to care for her or
give a friendly word in her behalf. Poor creature, she had given birth to a child in the woods,
being compelled to wander about like a wild
beast in the forest on account of the inhuman
treatment of the white man in this Bible land
of ours! Just you imagine the poor creature,
a precious soul in the sight of God, no doubt,
this temple of the living God, being driven by
blood-hounds, bruised and mangled as she
marched before them. And with all that she
was carried home and put in stocks at night
and beaten *every* morning. On being asked
how she got on in the woods without any
human help she said, " I don't know ; all I
can tell you, God took care of me."

Dear Christian reader, can we doubt the presence of God with her? Did he not say, "Lo, I am with you alway, even unto the end?" He has promised to guide us safely home if we will only follow him. Surely "He is a Rock in a weary land!" Glory be to God for all of his precious promises. Hattie could have cried out:

"But with thee is mercy found,
Balm to heal my every wound;
Soothe, O soothe this troubled breast,
Give the weary wanderer rest."

Aunt Lorendo's visits proved a source of much pleasure, as did Aunt Charlotte's many welcome visits.

CHAPTER XI.

PRISON HORRORS.

Uncle John taking lessons—Andersonville horrors—Blood-
hounds—Silas bitten by blood-hounds and eaten by buzzards.

UNCLE JOHN always made it a habit to
stop in on Saturday evenings. He was a
steward of his church, and as he could not
read very well he said he had made up his
mind to study and try to learn more. He
wanted to learn to read the Bible and hymn-
book, anyhow, he said. He had to lead
prayer-meeting in his church very often, and
he said it would do him so much good if he
could only read his Bible and hymn-book; so
he employed me to teach him. I must confess Uncle John was pretty hard to teach.
His mind was blunted, no doubt, and, having
to work hard every day, and old and feeble as
he was, I did not expect much of him. He
decided that the first thing I must do was to
read a chapter in the Bible, and also to read

a hymn, saying he wanted to get them "by heart." His favorite hymns were : " Show pity, Lord," " How firm a foundation," " Must I be to judgment brought?" and " Try us, O God."

He would say: " La, Mrs. A., if I only had these good times in my young days ! But I tell you, ma'am, I am glad I'm blest to see freedom ! How many of my poor people died in slave-time and never knowed nothing but hard work all their life-time ! I know," he said, " my poor Nancy is dead, and buried somewhere in Georgia. She worked hard all of her life-time, for the white folks never knowed what rest was. Sometimes I dream of all of my people I left in Georgia. It seems I can see my mammy in my sleep, and she comes right up beside my bed and talks with me sometimes. I know she is in heaven, for she used to be always talking about heaven when I was with her."

I said : " It would afford you so much joy to see your children once more ; I reckon they are still living."

He said : " Yes, ma'am ; I reckon if they is still living they is all married ; but the white folks was so bad in slave-time I expect they all is dead. They used to run black people down with nigger-hounds, and would let the dogs bite them all over."

"Yes, Uncle John; your wife spent several hours not long ago telling of a poor woman that lived there near her plantation who was caught by the dogs, and she said the last she saw of the woman she was bleeding from dog-bites."

"Yes, ma'am; the white folks was bad here in Louisiana, but I think they was worse in Georgia for blood-hounds."

"Why, Uncle John," I said, "it looks as if allowing the dogs to bite them would bring on hydrophobia, and thereby cause a great many deaths among the slaves?"

"Yes; they did die often; but I always thought they died from being worked to death. Why, ma'am, I have seen poor colored men bleeding and dying from dog - bites. Once right in Georgia I saw a man where he crawled 'way off from his plantation and died under a shade-tree. Madam, that poor man had iron around his feet when we found him, and the buzzards had almost eaten his body up. I knowed the poor man; his name was Silas.

He had run away and was caught by the dogs one morning, and his marster came up to him while he was fighting with the dogs, and Silas give one ·dog a blow and almost killed him. The hound was one of the best ones his marster had.   Madam, Silas's marster got off of his horse right there where they caught him and beat Silas with his pistol all over for nothing because he would not let the dog bite him. He made the dogs bite Silas all over his body. The dogs bit him under the throat.   When he got Silas home he put him in irons, but Silas could not walk.   Silas was almost dead when his marster put the irons on him.''

Uncle John said: ''Poor Silas ! I will never forget how I went out one Sunday morning and found him laying dead under that big oak-tree.   He had a wife and six or seven children. He lived on one of the plantations in Georgia. We used to go to church on Sundays together. O, how he used to love that hymn, ' How firm a foundation ! ' He knowed every word of it by heart,'' said Uncle John.   '' We used to hear the white people sing it at church.''

I asked Uncle John if Silas's master allowed him to attend church, and he said :

"Why, yes, ma'am; he used to let his slaves go to church on Sunday, and he went too; but that did not keep our white people from beating us through the week. They took sacrament in the morning, and we colored people took it in the evening."

"You were never allowed to take the sacrament with your masters?"

"No, ma'am; we been always separated here, and I reckon when we get up yonder in glory they will want to be separated," said Uncle John.

"No; there is no separation in glory. We read in the third chapter of Galatians, twenty-sixth to twenty-eighth verses: 'For ye are all the children of God by faith in Christ Jesus. For as many of you as have been baptized into Christ have put on Christ. There is neither Jew nor Greek, there is neither bond nor free, there is neither male nor female: for ye are all one in Christ Jesus.' Thus you see and hear what the Bible says: 'We are all one.'

  "'God is faithful; he will never
  Break his covenant sealed in blood;
  Signed when our Redeemer died;
  Sealed when he was glorified.'"

"Well," said Uncle John, "how in the world could the whites know the word of God, and so many used to seem to have religion, and yet treat us poor people just like the brutes?"

"I fear that a very few slave-holders had religion, Uncle John. If they had any at all it was not the Bible religion. Nevertheless, I do say there were some good white people who did not brutalize their slaves. But I regret to say that there were very few. They would punish them in many ways. If they did not kill them outright they killed them by brutalizing them. And we know that no murderers can enter that ' rest ' prepared for the people of God unless they repent."

"They used to go to church," said Uncle John, "in Georgia, and I have seen them happy, too; but, madam, they would come right back from church and beat us all the week and make us work ourselves nearly to death."

"Uncle John, that was inconsistent with the teaching of the Bible. The Spirit of God is love, peace, joy, and contentment."

"Madam, I have talked so long this evening I will not say my lessons; but will you please read that hymn I love so much?"

"'How firm a foundation,' Uncle John?"

"Yes, ma'am."

"Here it is:

"'How firm a foundation, ye saints of the Lord,
Is laid for your faith in his excellent word!
What more can he say, than to you he hath said,
To you, who for refuge to Jesus have fled?

"'Fear not, I am with thee, O be not dismayed,
For I am thy God, I will still give thee aid;
I'll strengthen thee, help thee, and cause thee to stand,
Upheld by my gracious, omnipotent hand.

"'When through the deep waters I call thee to go,
The rivers of sorrow shall not overflow;
For I will be with thee thy trials to bless,
And sanctify to thee thy deepest distress.

"'When through fiery trials thy pathway shall lie,
My grace, all-sufficient, shall be thy supply,
The flames shall not hurt thee; I only design
Thy dross to consume, and thy gold to refine.

"'E'en down to old age all my people shall prove
My sovereign, eternal, unchangeable love;
And when hoary hairs shall their temples adorn,
Like lambs they shall still in my bosom be borne.

"'The soul that on Jesus hath leaned for repose,
I will not, I will not desert to his foes;
That soul, though all hell shall endeavor to shake,
I'll never, no never, no never forsake!'"

Uncle John said: "O, bless the Lord! how often I heard that hymn sung in Georgia! Silas, poor man, did love it too. Madam, I do believe the angels came for Silas that day he crawled out under that big oak-tree and died there. You remember I told you we lived 'joining plantations, and many times I used to see him on his knees praying and praising God at twelve o'clock in the cotton-field. O, yes; I expect to meet Silas high up in glory!"

"Uncle John, I've often heard and read of Andersonville, Georgia, where so many Union soldiers were imprisoned during the war. I've been informed that blood-hounds were kept to chase the prisoners who escaped the stockade."

"Yes, madam; I know a man near this place now that came from Georgia about four years ago, and he lived somewhere near Andersonville in the time of the war. Madam, that man would make you cry if you could hear him tell how the white people used to make the blood-hounds chase the Yankees at that stockade in Andersonville, Georgia. He told me they had blood-hounds all around Andersonville."

"Uncle John, what is the man's name?"

"He is named Samson Jones. Madam, Samson said they had a big dog-kennel where they kept the dogs to chase the Yankees. They run them all through the woods whenever one escaped from the stockade. He told me he had seen many Yankees bitten almost to death by the blood-hounds. He said they used to get out of the stockade and run just like we poor darkies did, with the dogs right behind them. He said the Yankees died like flies in prison, and that he was one of the colored men that helped to bury them there."

"Brother Samson is from Georgia, and he knows all about the Andersonville stockade. So I suppose that his account of the stockade is certainly true?"

"Yes, madam, I believe he is reliable. He told me the wagons used to run night and day burying the prisoners in the warm season. I tell you, madam, Samson could talk all day to you about what he has seen in that stockade at Andersonville, Georgia. He told me thousands of Yankees were walled up in the stockade made of pine-trees, and they had no shed over them. The hot sun used to almost

7

parch them. The rain would pour down on them, and they were shut up like cows in a pasture."

"I've said already, Uncle John, I've read of the horrors of Andersonville; but how strange that these things should be in the State of Georgia, where religion abounds, and where the Gospel was preached Sunday after Sunday, within hearing, perhaps, of the stockade, and that thousands of human souls should receive such brutal treatment!"

They were reduced to a level with the brutes, the barren earth for a floor and the sky their only covering overhead! Samson said the white women used to visit the stockade. They had a platform made so they could walk out and look over the stockade down on the prisoners; and one time a white woman said, when she was looking over at them, "I wish God would rain fire and brimstone down on your heads." Samson said he heard her say it to the Yankees. There they were, dumb and helpless, some dead, some dying, and others almost starved to death. And a Christian woman, so called, cried out to them, "I wish God would rain fire and brimstone down

on your heads!" My Lord and my God, we
prostrate ourselves before thee and cry, Where
are we? In a Christian land? O, that bloody
spot, Andersonville! Thy name shall never
be erased from the annals of history. The
thirteen thousand and seven hundred souls
that are now sleeping beneath thy sod, and
the hundreds of others that perished in the
swamps that surround thee, will rise up in the
judgment and condemn thee. Let us thank
God and sing:

> " Shout, for the foe is destroyed that inclosed thee,
> The oppressor is vanquished, and Zion is free ! "

Not only the bloody ground at Andersonville will condemn the Christians in these
Southern States in the general judgment, but
what must we say of the millions of poor, innocent slaves that have been murdered here in
this Christian land for two hundred and fifty
years! "Their blood be upon you and your
children!" "Cry aloud, spare not, lift up
thy voice like a trumpet, and show my people
their transgression, and the house of Jacob
their sins."

CHAPTER XII.

SALLIE SMITH'S STORY.

Sallie Smith living in the woods—Death of her mother—The ill-treatment she suffered.

THE subject of this sketch is another faithful sister of Aunt Charlotte's church. She was born in the State of Louisiana, on Bayou Bœuf. As I had the pleasure of meeting her very often, and, seeing she manifested much interest and real devotion for her church, I became much attached to her. So once as she passed I asked her, if it was not unpleasant to her, if she would please spend a while with me and tell the story of her life as a slave.

She readily assented, saying: " Yes, my dear child. There aint a day but what I think how good my blessed Jesus has been to me and all of my people. O, sometimes I think of my old slave-days, and begin to cry for joy when I remember how good the Lord has been to me. Well do I remember when my poor mother died and left me and my little brother. .She

called us as she was about to die, and said, 'My
dear children, I am going to leave you. The
angels is waiting for me. I am almost over.
Promise me you will follow me.' I said,
' Mother, is you going to leave us?' and before
she could answer she was dead. Madam, I
cried night and day ; it seemed my mother's
death would nearly kill me. We was slaves,
and had nobody to care any thing for us. We
both had to work hard just like the others on
the place. I was about fourteen, and my
brother about one year old. The overseer got
mad whenever he saw me cry. He told me to
hush crying, and said, 'Your mother is dead
and in hell, and could not come back here ; and
if you don't hush I'll beat you half to death.'
He was a Catholic, and hated my mother's sort
of religion. When he said my mother was in
hell that made me cry more ; and he beat me
and kicked me all 'round in the field. I had to
pick one hundred and fifty pounds of cotton
every day or get a whipping at night.''

" Were you always able to get one hundred
and fifty pounds every day? "

" No, my child, I could not. Sometimes
I'd pick it, but I could not get it every day.

One night I got up just before day and run away; and I tell you I stayed in the woods one half of my time. Sometimes I'd go so far off from the plantation I could not hear the cows low or the roosters crow."

"Where did you sleep at night, and how did you get something to eat?"

"I slept on logs. I had moss for a pillow; and I tell you, child, I wasn't scared of nothing. I could hear bears, wild-cats, panthers, and every thing. I would come across all kinds of snakes—moccasin, blue runner, and rattle-snakes—and got used to them. One night while I was in the woods a mighty storm came up; the winds blowed, the rain poured down, the hail fell, the trees was torn up by the roots, and broken limbs fell in every direction; but not a hair on my head was injured, but I got as wet as a drowned rat. Next day was a beautiful Sunday, and I dried myself like a buzzard."

"Aunt Sallie, you did not tell me how you got your meals."

"O, child, sometimes I did not get any; but many time I'd find out where the hands on the place were working, and if the overseer was

away I'd get something from them.   They
would bring me something, too, after they
found out where I was, and I'd wait on the edge
of the woods every day ; and when they would
come to hunt for me they called out in a low,
piercing sound, ' Sallie, Sallie ! '   I'd come running, and sometimes I was nearly perished."

"Why, Aunt Sallie, it seems to me it was
far better for you to have stayed at home than
to wander about in the woods."

" No, I could not stay after my mother died.
The overseer was mean to me.   He beat me
every day, and I had no kin on the plantation
but my brother, and he could do nothing for
me.   I got used to staying in the woods, and
felt satisfied there.   I had a flint-rock and piece
of steel, and I could begin a fire any time I
wanted.   Sometimes I'd get a chicken and
would broil it on the coals and would bake
ash-cake.

" I remember one night," said Aunt Sallie,
" I went to the quarters and knocked at the
door of one old lady that belonged to my marster, and she let me in.   I asked her for something to eat, but she said, ' I aint got a piece
of bread done, but if you want you can bake

you a corn-cake.' And bless your soul, child,
just as I was about to cook my bread the overseer came in and caught me. La, me! I
thought I'd faint when he came in the door."

"Well, what did he do with you?"

"He tied me with a rope by both arms and
carried me to the smoke-house. When he got
in he throwed the rope over the joist of the
smoke-house and left me there all night. He
just allowed my toes to touch the floor when
he tied me up by my wrists. But, my child,
the Lord was with me that night! I managed
to get my wrists out of the rope and I sat up
nodding in the smoke-house all that night. I
was afraid to let him see me down, so just as he
was about to unlock the door the next day I
slipped my hands back in the rope. He
thought I had been tied all night; but, bless
the Lord! I was just like Paul and Silas when
they were in jail. I cried to the Lord and he
loosened the rope. Madam, although I did not
have religion when I used to live in the woods,
yet it seemed I could not keep from praying.
I'd think of my mother, how, just before she
died, she told me to 'come.' And that word
always followed me. I used to lie out in the

woods on the logs, with moss under my head,
and pray a many and many a night. I hardly
knowed what to say or how to pray, but I re-
membered how I used to hear my mother
praying, on her knees, in the morning before
day, long before she died, and I just tried to
say what she used to say in her prayers. I
heard her say many a time, ' O, Daniel's God,
look down from heaven on me, a poor, needy
soul !' I would say, 'O, Daniel's God, look
down from heaven on me in these woods !'
Sometimes it seemed I could see my mother
right by my side as I laid on the log asleep.
One time I talked with her in my sleep. I
asked her, 'Mother, are you well?' And it
seemed I could hear her saying, as she beck-
oned to me, ' Come, O come; will you come?'
And I did try to get up in my sleep and start
to her, and I rolled off the log. By that time
I woke up, and the sun was shining clear and
bright and I was there to wander about in the
woods?"

"You have not told me what he did with
you when he took you out of the smoke-house
that morning."

" Why, he had a big barrel he kept to roll us

in, with nails drove all through it, and he put
me in it and had a man to roll me all over the
yard. Madam, I thought he was going to kill
me. When the overseer had me taken out of
that barrel I could hardly walk. I was sore
and bruised all over. That night a poor old
woman on our place greased me all over, and
I got over with the bruises and went to work."

"Well, I suppose that was an end to your
stay in the woods?"

"No, madam, I did not stay more than a
month before I ran away again. I tell you, I
could not stay there. I had got used to the
woods, and the overseer was so brutal to me.
The weather was beginning to turn cold, and I
made me a moss bed just like a hog, and I kept
warm at night. But many times I used to
sleep in the chimney-corners on a plantation
next to my marster's. I could hear the colored
people inside the cabins pray and sing at
night."

"Why, it seems you could have gone inside
the cabins and stayed with them, Aunt Sallie?"

"Well, yes, I did go in often, but they
finally told me I must stop coming. They said
the overseer on their place would beat them to

death if he caught me in their cabins. So
I stopped going inside. They did not know I
was outside of the chimney. I heard them
sing many times this hymn:

> " ' In the morning when I rise,
> In the morning when I rise,
> In the morning when I rise,
> Give me Jesus, give me Jesus,
> Give me Jesus!
> You may have all this world;
> Give me Jesus!' "

CHAPTER XIII.

IN THE WOODS.

Aunt Sallie's cruel treatment, continued—Her brother Warren runs away and joins her in the woods.

"THE next time I ran away I met my brother, who had run away two or three weeks before the overseer caught me that night. He told me the overseer beat him so much he could not work. Because I ran away he said my brother knew where I was. My brother's name is Warren. Poor Warren! when he met me that morning he was scarred all over. The overseer told him he had to find me or he would almost skin him. So Warren left the place; but I hadn't seen him in two months, I reckon, till I met him that morning. We sat all day long talking over what we had better do. Warren said, ' Sallie, let me tell you what's best for us to do. You know old Uncle Tim says he can houdoo and make the white folks stop doing us so bad, and let us do what he told us. Let us get some of the white folks' hair and some salt and a piece of old mistress's dress, and make a little bag and sew it up and put it under the steps where all the white folks have to pass over every day. Uncle Tim says it will make the white folks stop treating us so bad. He says when we go to put it under the steps we must say as we throw it, ' Malumbia, Malumbia, peace I want, and peace I must have, in the name of the Lord.' "

" Aunt Sallie, what does Malumbia mean ? "

" La, madam, I don't know what it meant. But Warren wanted me to fix the bag and put it under them white folks' steps, but I thought it best to stay in the woods."

" Who is Uncle Tim ? "

" He was an old man that stayed around the yard to wait on the white folks and take care of the horses and cow. He first came from Africa. He said he used to eat folks in Africa. He could not talk good like we all could. He came from South Carolina to Louisiana, when my marster bought him. Uncle Tim had relig-ion, and I used to hear him say, when he would be talking to my mother, ' Me lover my Lord like my Lord lover me ; me *never eater poor soul* no more.' I don't even remember when he came to Louisiana. It was long before I was born; but I heard people say he was right from Africa to this country. We all used to call him 'Uncle Summer-time' and he liked that name. He was a good old man, but he believed in houdoo. O, yes; no doubt they were heathen habits that he learned in his native land. I used to hear him many times, when he would be down on his knees praying, say, 'O, Shadrach, Meshach, Abed-Negroes' God blesses poor Summer-time's soul!' and then he would stop still and holler out, 'O, how me loves my Lord like my Lord loves me!' Although I was young I will never forget Uncle Tim Summer-time."

"Aunt Sallie, what did you and your brother decide upon in the woods!"

"O, we wandered about in the woods, I don't know how long. We would pick berries to eat, and would get any thing we came upon. I told Warren about my dream of our mother, and that I saw her come up to me, and that I had been praying every night on my moss bed. I wanted to get him to pray too. I said to him, 'Warren, you know how our poor mother used to pray way before day in the morning,

and how we used to hear her cry and say, " O,
Daniel's God, have mercy on me!" And it
makes me feel glad every time I pray, Warren ;
and now let us pray every time before we go to
sleep.' Warren said, 'Well, let us pray to
Daniel's God just like our poor mother did.'
And we did every night before we went to
sleep, after wandering all through the woods
all day. Me and Warren would pray. We
prayed low and easy; we just could hear each
other. Warren used to pray, ' O, Daniel's
God, have mercy on me and Sallie. Mother
said you will take care of us, but we suffer here;
nobody to help us. Hear us way up in
heaven and look down on us here.' Madam,
we did not know hardly what to say, but we
had heard mother and other people praying,
and we tried to do the best we could. Sometimes we was so hungry we could hardly sleep,
and it would be so cold, too, we did not know
what to do. We had a big heap of moss, and
we made a brush arbor over it to keep the rain
off. I took Warren to the same place where I
had been going at night in the chimney-corners to keep warm. But, la, madam, one morning we overslept ourselves and the overseer of

that plantation caught us. He carried us home
to old mistress. I heard her tell old marster
to not to let the overseer hit us a lick. She
said, 'Send them to the kitchen and give them
a plenty to eat and stop whipping them, and
see if you can't do more with them.' Madam,
I tell you when I overheard her talking to
marster tears came in my eyes. I told Warren.
O, how glad we felt that morning! I cried for
joy.

"After they gave us something to eat they let
us rest awhile. Me and Warren went to our
house and we talked how mistress looked like
she was sorry for us when she saw us just come
out of the woods that morning. We hardly
ever saw her, for we lived in quarters and the
house was away off. I told Warren Daniel's
God had heard us praying in the woods, and I
said, 'Warren, let us keep on praying and
trusting in God.' I said, 'You know the
overseer used to beat us whenever he caught
us, and roll me in the barrel, tie me up by my
waist-band, and punish us all sorts of ways.'
But this morning he got us and did not give
us a lick, but gave us a good breakfast and
sent us out here to rest. Madam, me and

Warren agreed right there not to give up praying night and day. We did follow our mother's rule. We would get up long before time to go to work to pray."

"So, Aunt Sallie, you did not believe in voudous?"

"No, ma'am. The next time I saw Uncle Tim I told him I did not believe in it. I said, ' Uncle Tim, I have been praying ever since my mother died, and you see the overseer don't do me as he used to. I tell you, Uncle Tim, Daniel's God heard me and Warren.' He told us to keep on praying; said, ' Daniel's God is a great God. He will hear his children when they cry.' He was a good old man, but we could not understand him much what he said, and he believed in houdoos."

"Yes, the vice of voudouism which is practiced among the colored people is the result of ignorance and slavery. They will, in the course of time, ignore such doctrine, for they are being educated, and the time will come when such simple and nonsensical teachings will find no place among them."

"Yes, ma'am; I believe they will learn better in the course of time."

"Well, tell me, Aunt Sallie, did you both finally remain at home after you were caught in the chimney-corner?"

"Yes, ma'am; we stayed after that. The overseer stopped doing us bad; but we had to work mighty hard to keep up. We both was blessed to see freedom. My brother is living right now in Springtown, and he comes to see me every Christmas. We both are soldiers for Jesus. He is a deacon in a Baptist church, and I am one of your noisy dry-land Methodists."

John's, and many others; but I've been told
so much about your history that I have long
craved to have you recite it yourself."

"Well, madam," said he, "I assure you that
my history has been a wonderful one. I tell
you, my dear child, nobody but God knows the
trouble we poor black folks had to undergo
in slave-time. My first old master was a
mighty good man, and my mistress used to
love me like her own children. In fact, my old
master was my own father; but, of course, the
thing was kept a sort of a secret, although
every body knew it. My mother was one of
the house servants, and I was raised about the
white folks' house. Indeed, after I was old
enough to be weaned old mistress had me to
sleep in a couch with her own children in her
own room, until I got to be a great big boy.
The children and I used to play together, and
after they began to go to school I used to go
with them to carry their books and lunch, and
they taught me every lesson they learned, so
that when I was about fourteen or fifteen years
old I could read and write as well as any of
them. But I tell you, child, this thing did not
last forever. Somehow or other old master

take place; and then he described the property to be sold, including the plantation, wagons, mules, cattle, and all the slaves. After
he had sold the plantation, wagons, mules,
horses, and cattle he began to sell the slaves.
Some were bought by neighboring planters,
some by the merchants and others that had
come from New Orleans, and others were
bought by negro traders to be placed in the
market and sold again. My mother was bought
by one of the New Orleans merchants; but I
was bought by a negro trader. My old mistress was sorry to part with me and a little pet
calf she had raised around the big house. So
she had us kept until the last to see if she
could not keep us; but old master's debts
could not be met after every thing else had
been sold, so the calf and I had to be sold.
The negro trader bought me and the calf together for five hundred and thirty dollars.
Next day all of us who had been sold to buyers living in and along the coast toward New
Orleans were shipped on a steam-boat going
that way. My mother was on that boat.
That night we reached New Orleans. Mother
was taken to her new owner's house to be a

house servant, and I was taken to the arcade,
or negro traders' yard. From that day until
peace was declared after the war I never laid
my eyes on my dear mother; that was nearly
twenty years. I tell you, people were miser-
able in that old slave-pen. Every day buyers
came and examined such slaves as they desired
to buy. They used to make them open their
mouths so that they could examine their teeth;
and they used to strip them naked, from head
to foot, to see whether they were perfectly
sound. And this they did to women as well
as men. I tell you, my dear child, it used to
seem to me so brutal to see poor women
treated in that way by brutal and heartless
men. I declare, child, I can't understand it,
although I've been right in it. When they
would put them naked that way they used to
switch them on the legs to make them jump
around so that buyers could see how supple
they were."

"I declare, Uncle Stephen, your story makes
me shudder."

"It was so, just as I tell you; but I did not
stay long in the negro traders' yard. I was
sold soon after that to a man that lived only a

few miles from the old place where I was raised
and sold from when mother and I was separated. My new master was a mighty mean
man, and would not allow any of his slaves to
go anywhere. He notified all the 'poor
'Cadien patrollers' to whip his slaves whenever
they caught any of them off the place."

"Who were these 'Cadien patrollers, Uncle
Stephen?"

"Why, child, they were the meanest things
in creation; they were poor, low down white
folks, that descended from a French and Spanish mixture. They had no slaves themselves,
and so they just took pleasure in patrolling the
public roads so as to get to whip somebody
else's slaves that happened to be out without
a pass."

"I had often heard that before; but I jus.
asked you to see whether what I had heard of
them was true."

"It is just so, child. They were a poor,
ignorant set that was just as mean as they
were poor and ignorant. The only advantage
they had over the negroes was that they were
white, that's all. Well, as I was going to tell
you, master would not allow his slaves to go

off the place. In order to keep them on the place he used to give them wives right on the place. He would not allow his slaves to take wives that did not belong to his plantation. Whenever he thought one of his men needed a wife or one of his women needed a husband he would choose them and put them together. If he did not own them he would go and buy a wife or a husband for those that he thought were old enough and needed them. He would never allow the men to be single after they were eighteen, nor the women after they were fifteen. I remember one day, when he had returned from town with about twenty-five heads of slaves, he called out all those who had no wives or husbands on the place. Said he, 'Well, boys, I've gotten a fine set of girls for you, and I am going to put you all together; likewise you, girls, I've got these fine boys, and I am going to put you all together, so that there will be no reason for any of you to have wives and husbands off the place. That old practice has got to stop;' so then he gave each one his wife or husband; he chose them out himself."

"Did he give you one, too, Uncle Stephen?"

CHAPTER XV.

COUNTERFEIT FREE PAPERS.

The overseer searches Uncle Stephen's cabin and finds his counterfeit free papers—His master about to kill him, but finally determines to sell him—Uncle Stephen's new master—His break for freedom and capture—His sentence to be hanged, and his freedom finally.

" UNCLE STEPHEN, what did you do with the wife your master gave you ? "

" Well, we stayed in the same cabin together, not as husband and wife, but as son and mother, she was so much older than I ; and I used to write out passes and slip them to her husband that lived on a neighboring plantation, so he could come and see her. But I tell you, child, things got to be so tight that I could not get to see my wife as often as I wanted ; so I made up my mind to run away. There was an old free negro that lived near our place ; I got him to let me see his free papers. I tell you, child, I took those free papers and copied every word of them. 'Now,' said I, ' I shall run away, and if I am caught I shall show these counterfeit free papers and get off all right.' Sure enough, I took those papers and stowed them away in a secret place in my cabin, together with my mother's picture and my own picture, which was taken when we belonged to Mr. Jordon, my first old master, together with some old passes, books, and papers. But one day, I don't know why, he suspected me. One of our slaves ran away, and the overseer was hunting for him. The overseer hunted every-where for him. While hunting for that runaway he went and searched my cabin ; finally he found my papers. When I found out that the overseer had found my papers and turned them over to my master I just made up my mind that I certainly would be killed. I tell you, child, the very thought makes my blood chill even now. It seemed like the news had gone out like wild-fire through the quarters that passes, free papers, and books had been found in 'poor Stephen's house,' and that old master was going to kill him. I had no sooner reached the big gate where I had gone to put up my mules in the stable than I heard the overseer cry out :

" 'Ah, Stephen ! your master is waiting for

you at the big house ; never mind about your
mules, but go right out to the house, where he
will make an eternal settlement with you.'

" ' There now,' said I, ' I am gone.' As I
stepped on the porch of the big house I saw
old master sitting in his dining-room with a
table before him. On the table were all of my
letters, old passes, free papers, newspapers,
books, and other papers, and by the side of
these old master had a fearful-looking dagger
and two army revolvers.

" ' Ah,' said he, ' you are the one that gives
passes to my niggers and makes free papers
for those who run away.' And he swore at
me.

" I tried to answer, but he was in such a
rage he would hear nothing. I thought he
would kill me every minute. Finally he said :

" ' Who taught you how to write ? I did
not know you were educated. Here you are,
better educated than any white man around
here. An educated nigger is a dangerous thing,
and the best place for him is six feet under
the ground, buried face foremost. Ah, sir,
your end is come, and you will not have use
for papers, books, and pens any longer.'

" I tell you, madam, I just made up my mind that my time had come and I would surely die. At last old master quieted a little, and I said :

" ' Master, I was raised in the house, and Master Jordon's children taught me how to read and write. But,' said I, ' I never wrote a free paper for any body in my life. True, I wrote those counterfeit free papers and put the name Sam in it, calling myself by that false name so that I might run away, because I could not get to see my old wife and children that live on Mr. François's place, but, master, I declare I never wrote free papers for any body in my life.'

" Of course I had written out the passes for the other slaves, but, although I knew it was a sin, to save myself I had to say that I just wrote the passes for pastime. How that man did not kill me I can't imagine, excepting that God would not let him. So he says to me :

" ' Your old master, Jordon, is to blame for this crime, and he ought to pay for it. That's the reason he is broke and don't own a dollar to-day ; but you can't stay here to spoil all my niggers ; you can't stay here another week.'

" I tell you, child, you can't imagine how

glad I was to get off so easy. I remained on
that place only two days after that, and then a
Mr. Valsin, that kept a big store, bought me
to work in his store.

"Mr. Valsin, my new master, seemed to be
ever so well pleased with me. His store was
in a thick settlement about fifteen miles up the
Mississippi River above my last master's plantation. I did all the work around the store,
and, as I was good at figuring and could read
and write, he had me to weigh out things and
to wait on many of the customers whenever he
needed me. I liked him very well, and I took
great interest in his business. Mr. Valsin had
a fair-sized plantation in connection with his
store, and owned about fifty head of slaves.
Generally he was a good man, but when angry
he was of a very violent temper. That is where
I was living about the time that the late civil
war began and when New Orleans fell into the
hands of the Union soldiers. But being about
twenty miles from where my wife was living,
and not being able to see or hear from her for
several years, I finally had to give up the hope
of ever seeing her again, and so I took up with
another woman that lived on our place. About

the time that General Butler captured New
Orleans slaves were running into the Union
line from all around our neighborhood. So
one day Mr. Valsin says to me,

" ' Well, Stephen, I suppose you will do like-
some of the other niggers, and run away from
me.'

" ' No, indeed,' said I, ' I shall never leave
you. Those Yankees are too bad, I hear.'

" ' That's so,' he said ; ' you will do much
better to stay with me and run off with us to
Texas before they get here.'

" Of course I liked Mr. Valsin well enough,
but I rather be free than be with him, or be
the slave of any body else. So his word about
going to Texas rather sunk deep into me, because I was praying for the Yankees to come
up our way just as soon as possible. I dreaded
going to Texas, because I feared that I would
never get free. The same thought was in the
mind of every one of the slaves on our place.
So two nights before we were to leave for
Texas all the slaves on our place had a secret
meeting at midnight, when we decided to leave
to meet the Yankees. Sure enough, about one
o'clock that night every one of us took through

others, but I was the educated one ; I was the one that had planned all this devilment, as he called it, and I was to be killed as an example for all the rest. For this I was sent away out to New Iberia, where I was placed in jail preparatory to my execution. Then the Yankees were coming so fast they decided to send me to Opelousas jail, where I was finally to suffer death for conspiring and assisting slaves to escape. While in this jail I waited every day for the time when I was to be hung until I was pronounced dead. The scaffold was built just outside the jail, and next day at twelve o'clock I was to die on that scaffold. But that very night, by some means or other that I've never been fully able to understand, I was bought by a man that lived in Texas. He, with the jailer, woke me up and took me out, and I was that very night shipped off to Texas, where I remained until the war was over and peace was declared. My Texas master, Mr. Maxwell, treated me very kindly, and when the war was over he told me that I was my own free man, and could go or stay just as I thought best. As he was a very clever kind of a man I contracted with him and worked

for him one year, after which I returned to the
city of New Orleans, where I was reunited to
my mother and my present wife, whom I married at Mr. Valsin's. My other wife had married, as I had also done during the long years
of our enforced and hopeless separation. The
children I had with her are now grown and
have entered upon the active duties of life.
Since that I have accumulated property and
have done some good, I hope, in the world,
and am now enjoying a happy and contented
old age.

"But I tell you, child, I was fortunate to
find my mother, my wife, and my children. So
many who were separated by slavery were never
reunited again in this world, and will never
meet again until they enter the eternal world."

"That's very true," said I; "but, Uncle
Stephen, haven't you heard of that wonderful
column in the *South-western Christian Advocate* called the 'Lost Friends' Column?' By
means of an advertisement in that column I
have heard of friends and relatives that long
had been separated being brought together.
Why, I suppose my husband could tell you of
several hundreds of such cases. One told me

the other day of her relatives whom she had left
in West Virginia years before the war ; another
of her relatives in South Carolina, whom they
had found by advertising in that column.   So I
have heard of others, whose relatives had been
left in Virginia, Maryland, Kentucky, Tennessee, Georgia, Mississippi, Texas, and, in fact, in
every Southern and other States, that thus
have been restored to each other.   I tell you,
these reunions must be seasons of great joy.   I
don't suppose there's any thing like it except
the glorious reunion in our Father's house
when life and its cares are all over ! ''

CHAPTER XVI.

UNCLE CEPHAS'S STORY.

Lizzie Beaufort would rather die than live a wicked life—Her
    brother Cato runs away, hides in the swamps, and finally
    makes his way to freedom by the aid of the Under-
    ground Railroad—Cato becomes a soldier, senator, and
    congressman—How Uncle Cephas learned to read,
    bought himself, and became a rich and honored citizen.

MY interest in, and conversations with,
    Aunt Charlotte, Aunt Sallie, Uncle John
Goodwin, Uncle Stephen, and the other characters represented in this story led me to in-
terview many other people that could give me
any additional facts and incidents about the
colored people, in freedom as well as in slavery.

Uncle Cephas, who used to live in Tennessee
before the war, and who came to Louisiana at
the close of the late war of the rebellion, told
me many things which I am sure would interest any one. He told me a very pathetic story
of a colored girl, eighteen years old, whose
master had bought her in South Carolina and
brought her to Tennessee. Her name was

Lizzie Beaufort. She was a most beautiful
girl. She had large black eyes, long black
hair, a beautiful oval-shaped face, and was of a
fine oily brunette complexion. She might have
easily passed for a Cuban; but she was the
slave of her own father, who had sold her to
this Tennessee planter. Her Tennessee master had bought her to be his kept woman, but
Lizzie declared that she would rather die a
thousand deaths than live such a life. She was
willing to work her hands off, and do any thing
that was required of her, but she just told her
master that he would have her to kill, but that
she never would submit to be made the instru-
ment of his hateful lust. It was of no use.
He coaxed, he pleaded, he threatened, and he
beat her, but Lizzie stood as firmly as a rock
against all his advances.

When he saw that he could not persuade her
by any means he determined to sell her. She
was sold to a negro trader, who brought her
out to Mississippi.

Uncle Cephas told me also the story of
Lizzie's brother, Cato, who made his way
from the rice-fields of South Carolina to
Canada about ten years before the war.

Uncle Cephas got the facts from Lizzie's own lips.

He said : "Lizzie told me all about it herself. Cato ran away and was gone over two months before they knew what had become of him. It took him all that time dodging in the swamps until he could make his way through the free States into Canada. But after he got to Canada he wrote back to a friendly white man that lived in the neighborhood, who told Lizzie and her mother all about it. The white man was from the North, and was very friendly to us colored people, but he had to be mighty careful about showing it, because all the white people suspicioned him, because they said he was a Northern man. He was the one that helped Cato to make his escape. It was good that he was not-found out, for they certainly would have killed him. He bargained with a ship-master to take Cato from Charleston to Boston. Cato was packed in a box and shipped for a box of cabbage. He was packed in the box with cabbage-leaves all around him, to make the box appear as a box of cabbage sure enough. The white man was an agent of what was then known as the Underground

Railroad. He notified the Underground Railroad people in Boston of the time when Cato would reach Boston, so that they might get him and run him off into Canada before he should be captured, if discovered, under the Fugitive Slave Act, which was then in force all over this country.

"The Lord was with Cato, however, and he reached Canada in safety. He fell in among good people there, and was soon doing well. He soon got a good education and plenty of property. When the war broke out he came back to Boston, joined the Union army, and came South and fought in some of the hardest battles of the war. A cousin of mine, who used to know Lizzie in Tennessee, met her near Vicksburg two years ago, and she told him that Cato was then living there, and was one of the greatest leaders of his race in Mississippi. He had been sheriff of his county, had been a senator, and had served his State in Congress and in several other stations of honor and trust."

"But," said I, "Uncle Cephas, you speak very properly for one that was a slave. You must have got an education notwithstanding the law against negroes being permitted to learn how to read and write."

" Ah, my child," said he, " my life has been an eventful one. It is true that slaves were not permitted to learn how to read ; but I was determined to learn if it was any way possible to do so. You see I was not born free, but my master and his wife died when I was only five years old. They were old people, and had no children ; so they left me and all my relatives free in their will. Notwithstanding that, how-ever, the will was contested in court and found defective, and we were all sold to satisfy claims against the estate. Mother was sold to a man that lived in Alabama, brother Jerry to one that lived in North Carolina, and sister Rachel to a negro trader that sold her to a family in Florida. I was sold to Judge S——, in Tennes-see. He was one of the most heartless men that ever lived. I can't begin to tell you of his meanness. I suppose if I had lived with him till the emancipation I would never have amounted to any thing, but, as the Lord would have it, he got broke by his senseless extrava-gance and was sold out at sheriff sale, and in that sale I was bought by Parson Winslow, a very kind-hearted old Methodist preacher. Parson told me that he did not buy me because he needed any slaves, but because he thought I had too good a turn to be made a dog of by such a heartless master. Parson Winslow knew me well, because whenever he came on his circuit in our neighborhood and stopped at our house I had to take care of his horse for him. After I had stayed with him about ten years one day he said to me: 'Cephas, I see you are a mighty smart boy, and seem to be making extra dimes by doing odd jobs around. I want to encourage your manly disposition. I want to fix it so you can buy yourself, your wife, and your children. What do you say to that?'

"Why, madam, that word went through me like lightning. I had saved some money for that very purpose, but never dared propose the matter to the parson. (We never called him any thing but parson. He wouldn't let us call him any thing else.) So as soon as he made the proposition I gladly accepted the offer.

"'But,' said I, 'parson, I'll never be able to pay you for myself, my wife, and my children. How can I?' 'Well,' said he, 'pay me twenty-

five dollars a month for your time, and whatever you make over that shall be yours.' I
had a very good trade ; I was a blacksmith
and machinist, and I could get two dollars
and a half a day for every working-day in
the year. I told Dinah, my wife, all about it,
and she was perfectly delighted. From that
on I worked and Dinah worked. We both
worked, and I tell you, madam, before many
more years passed over my head I had bought
myself, Dinah, and our two children.

" All the years I was at the parson's I was
never without a book or paper about me. His
children used to teach me on the sly when
they came to see Dinah. Dinah was the cook,
and a mighty good one she was, too. After I
was free I just made good for lost time and
learned all I could, so that when the war came
on I was a pretty good scholar. I was not
satisfied to see myself free and make no efforts
to help others of my race. Having such a
good trade and a plenty of work I made plenty
of money and saved it. Dinah, too, was a
very smart woman. So by her help and the
help of our two boys we could always lay our
hands on several hundred dollars in hard cash.

With that I bought poor slaves, I can scarcely tell you how many. I would buy them and then give them time to pay me. When they worked and paid me what I paid for them I would give them their free papers. Let's see, I did that for Jim Sanders, who was a very smart man, and who after the war became Secretary of State in his adopted State; for Frank Shorter, who became a member of Congress, and a number of others. These, however, were exceptionally brilliant men, and lost no time in pushing themselves right to the front. Jim, I believe, is still a senator, and has been in one branch or another of the Legislature of his State for the last twenty years. Of course I can't help from calling them Jim and Frank, I know them so well. Jim lives in Louisiana, and Frank lives in South Carolina. In fact, every one I helped in that way proved to be of the best metal. Nearly all of them were active in the reconstruction of their States, were in the constitutional conventions, the legislatures, etc.; and but for the suppression of negro majorities in the South I suppose many of them would still be felt as great political agencies in this country. Several of them, however, like myself, are growing old, and are leading a quiet home-life; and then others of them have died and gone the way of all the earth. I never cared about politics myself, however. I never thought our salvation depended so much upon politics. Education, property, and character, to my mind, have ever been the trinity of power to which I have looked and do look for our complete redemption in this country. No earthly power can undermine and destroy the progress of a people thus intrenched. With that principle in me, I have ever tried to regulate my practice accordingly. I educated both of my sons and gave them each a good trade. One of them, however, is now a physician in Texas, and the other is pastor of one of the largest churches in Washington, D. C. He graduated with high honors at one of the best theological schools in this country, and is to-day a recognized authority in Greek, Hebrew, and the Shemitic languages. They are both good boys, and Dinah and I are proud of them. I like to recall and talk over such matters; they stir up all the enthusiasm of my younger days."

It would have done you good to have heard

CHAPTER XVII.

A COLORED SOLDIER.

Colonel Douglass Wilson on the war—Color-bearer Planchiancio and Captain Caillioux—Joel Brinkley, a Yankee
school-teacher, caned nearly to death.

AFTER my conversation with Uncle Cephas in the last chapter I did not get to
see any one particularly for a month or more
who could add materially to my story any thing
that might interest you ; but during the succeeding summer, after this last conversation, I
met Colonel Douglass Wilson, a colored man
of considerable prominence, not only in Louisiana, but in the nation. He and his family
and my husband, daughter, and I were spending a vacation at Bay St. Louis, Mississippi,
a very popular watering-place on the Mississippi Sound. He and my husband were very
great friends, and used to visit each other during our stay there. One day I said to him :

"Colonel, from what I have heard you say
and learned of you generally, as a public man,

you must have a rich experience touching oc-
currences before, during, and since the war
among our people. I have made the matter
one of deep study, and I know your story
would delight almost any one. Don't keep
all the good things to yourself; tell us about
them sometime."

"Yes," said he, "my experience is a rich
and varied one, and I am so constantly telling
it every-where and on every occasion that I
fear sometimes that people will say that I
have a hobby."

" I assure you," said I, "you will never hear
that from me, because I believe we should not
only treasure these things, but should transmit
them to our children's children. That's what
the Lord commanded Israel to do in reference
to their deliverance from Egyptian bondage,
and I verily believe that the same is his will
concerning us and our bondage and deliverance in this country. After thirty-three centuries the Jews are more faithful in the observance of the facts connected with their bondage
and deliverance than we are in those touching ours, although our deliverance took place
scarcely a quarter of a century ago."

"You are right, Mrs. Albert," replied the colonel, "and that is my principal reason for so heartily concurring with those of our leading colored men who are doing all in their power to induce all of our people in this country to unite every year in the observance of January 1 as National Emancipation Day. There can be no doubt that that is the day every true American should celebrate as National Emancipation Day, as that was the day on which Mr. Lincoln's ever-memorable proclamation of freedom was issued—January 1, 1863."

"Colonel, let me ask you, were you ever a slave?"

"A slave? Why, yes; I was a slave until Mr. Lincoln's proclamation of freedom. It found me, however, on the battle-field at Port Hudson, La., where the colored troops fought so nobly as to extort from their chief officers such praises as were showered upon few soldiers at any time or place. I was there in the hottest of the fight, when Captain Caillioux, that valiant negro, fell, one whose praises can never be too loudly proclaimed. If ever patriotic heroism deserved to be honored in stately marble or in brass that of Captain Caillioux

10

deserves to be, and the American people will have never redeemed their gratitude to genuine patriotism until that debt is paid. I was there, yes, ma'am, when, with one arm dangling in his sleeve, the brave captain waved his comrades on to the bloody conflict with the other. I was there, too, and heard the lion-hearted color-bearer, Planchiancio, when he received the regimental colors from his superior officer, and, grasping them with a firm and manly hand, assured him that he would ' return with those colors from the sweeping, bloody fray with honor, or report to God the reason why.' The recital of these things fires all the military ardor in my soul. From that day to the close of the war ' Remember Port Hudson ' was the talismanic watchword that ever inspired our regiment to the highest degree of heroism. But Port Hudson was only one of a hundred battle-fields whereon the colored soldier demonstrated his valor. There were Fort Pillow, Fort Wagner, Chickamauga, Fort Blakely, Fort Donelson, Lake Providence, Pulaski, Waterproof, Appomattox, and a hundred others. The verdict was that ' the colored troops fought nobly.'

the South, were a very aged man and his wife.
The slaves were escaping from the old plantations in every direction. So one morning a
planter out near Vicksburg, Miss., went out
into his negro quarters, and, addressing this
aged patriarch, now bent under the weight of
over threescore and ten years, said, 'Uncle
Si, I don't suppose you are going off to those
hateful Yankees, too, are you?' 'O no, marster,' he said, 'I'se gwine to stay right here
with you.' Next morning the planter visited
the quarters again, when he found that every
one of his slaves, not excepting even Uncle Si
and his wife, Aunt Cindy, had gone to the
Yankees during the night. Searching out in
the woods for them, he finally came upon Uncle
Si, just inside the Union line. Aunt Cindy
was stretched out on the bare ground, dead,
and Uncle Si was bending over her, weeping.
She had died from the exposure and hardship
incident upon the making of their escape.
Addressing Uncle Si, the planter said, 'Uncle
Si, why on earth did you so cruelly bring Aunt
Cindy here for, through all of such hardship,
thereby causing her death?' Lifting up his
eyes and looking his master full in the face, he

answered, 'I couldn't help it, marster; but then, you see, she died free.'"

"Colonel, tell me something about the Kuklux. Did you know any thing about them? They were said to be very bad and numerous in Georgia and South Carolina."

"That's true; at that time they were very bad and numerous in both Georgia and South Carolina, but they were equally bad in Louisiana, Mississippi, Texas, and, in fact, throughout the South. They were known in some places as the White Camelias, the White Cohort, and other such names, but after all they were nothing more nor less than the Confederate army that had surrendered at Appomattox that was really continuing a sort of guerrilla warfare against Union men and the poor freedmen. This was what made the task of reconstruction such a difficult one throughout the South. The Kuklux were determined that the colored people, if now free, should not enjoy their freedom, but should remain in a condition of peonage. To accomplish their purpose they heaped all sorts of indignities upon the northern white missionary preachers and teachers that followed the march of the Union lines to

organize our people in church relations and to
establish schools among them.   Not only were
they socially ostracized, but they were mal-
treated, whipped, mobbed, and massacred by
wholesale.

"I remember, just now, the case of Mr. Joel
Brinkley, who was taken out of his school-
house, right before his scholars, in broad day-
time, and caned half to death by a mob of
nearly a hundred of those hyenas.   After that
they gave him five hours in which to leave
the town of Springdale, where he was teaching.   After he started off they thought they
ought to have killed him, so they started off
after him to catch him, and they followed him
for ten days, trying to catch him.   He had to
hide in the swamps, sleep in the cane-rows
and ditches and under negro cabins to save his
life.   A reward of five hundred dollars was offered for his apprehension and delivery into
their hands, but the Lord was with him, and
he finally reached New Orleans in safety, where
he could continue in the same line of work with
a little more security.   I have often heard him
tell of how kindly the colored people treated
him when he was then fleeing for his life.

They were the only friends he could trust. They would hide him under their cabins and in their hay-lofts, and feed him there until it was safe for him to journey on farther. From them, too, he could learn of the whereabouts of the human hounds that were pursuing him for his life. Mr. Brinkley, however, was fortunate to have gotten away with his life, notwithstanding the fact that he thereby contracted terrible constitutional troubles, from which he suffered many years. Hundreds of others were killed outright, their churches or school-houses burnt down, and their families driven away. They were equally murdered, however, some instantly, while others, like Mr. Brinkley, died a slower death."

CHAPTER XVIII.

NEGRO GOVERNMENT.

Kuklux—Reign of terror—Black laws—Reconstruction—
Colored men in constitutional conventions and State legislatures—Lieutenant-Governor Dunn—Honest Antoine
Dubuclet—Negro problem—What the race has accom-
plished since the war—Emigration and colonization.

" IF the Kuklux treated the missionaries
in that manner you must not imagine
that they left the colored people and their
children unharmed. Thousands of colored
men and women throughout the South were in
like manner whipped and shot down like dogs,
in the fields and in their cabins. The recital
of some of the experiences of those days is
enough to chill your blood and raise your hair
on ends. The horrors of those days can
scarcely be imagined by those who know nothing about it. Why, madam, you ought to have
been down here in 1868. That was the year
in which Grant and Colfax ran for President
and Vice-President, against Seymour and Blair.
A perfect reign of terror existed all over the

pelt them with stones and run them down with open knives, both to and from school. Sometimes they came home bruised, stabbed, beaten half to death, and sometimes quite dead. My own son himself was often thus beaten. He has on his forehead to-day a scar over his right eye which sadly tells the story of his trying experience in those days in his efforts to get an education. I was wounded in the war, trying to get my freedom, and he over the eye, trying to get an education. So we both call our scars marks of honor. In addition to these means to keep the negro in the same servile condition I was about to forget to tell you of the 'black laws,' which were adopted in nearly all of the Southern States under President Andrew Johnson's plan of reconstruction. They adopted laws with reference to contracts, to the movement of negro laborers, etc., such as would have made the condition of the freed negro worse than when he had a master before the war. But, in the words of General Garfield upon the death of President Lincoln, 'God reigns, and the government at Washington still lives.' It did live, and, notwithstanding Andrew Johnson, it lived under the divine

supervision which would not and did not allow
the Southern States to reconstruct upon any
such dishonorable, unjust plan to the two hundred thousand negro soldiers who offered their
lives upon the altar for the perpetuation of the
Union and the freedom of their country. And
the whole matter was repudiated by Congress,
and the States were reconstructed upon the
plan of equal rights to every citizen, of whatever race or previous condition. It was then
declared that, whereas the stars on our national
flag had been the property of only the white
race and the stripes for only the colored, now
the stars should forever be the common property of both, and that the stripes should only
be given to those that deserved them.

"Under this new plan of reconstruction
many colored men entered the constitutional
conventions of every Southern State; and in
the subsequent organization of the new State
governments colored men took their seats
in both branches of the State governments,
in both Houses of Congress, and in all the
several branches of the municipal, parochial,
State, and national governments. It is true
that many of them were not prepared for such

a radical and instantaneous transition. But I tell you, madam, it was simply wonderful to see how well they did. And although in the midst of prejudice and partisan clamor a great deal of the most withering criticisms have been spent upon the ignorance, venality, and corruption of the negro carpet-bag reconstruction govern- ments inaugurated by our people, I believe time will yet vindicate them, and their achieve- ments will stand out in the coming years as one of the marvels of the ages. Who of all the officers of any State government can compare with the unassuming, dignified, and manly Oscar J. Dunn, Louisiana's first negro lieuten- ant-governor, or with Antoine Dubuclet, her honest and clean-handed treasurer for twelve years? His successor, E. A. Burke, a white man, representing the virtue and intelligence of our 'higher civilization,' is to-day a fugitive from the State for having robbed that same treasury of nearly a million dollars. Alabama has had her Vincent, Tennessee her Polk, Mis- sissippi her Hemingway, Kentucky, Maryland, and nearly every one of the Southern States have had their absconding State treasurers, with hundreds of thousands of dollars of the peo-

just what you think of our future in this country, anyway. Tell me whether we are pro-
gressing or retrograding, and whether you
think it is necessary for us to emigrate to
Africa or to be colonized somewhere, or what?"

"Well, madam, I must confess that some of
your questions are extremely hard to answer.
Indeed, some of them are to-day puzzling some
of the profoundest philosophers and thinkers
in this country; and I doubt very much
whether I could assume to answer them dog-
matically. One thing, however, I can tell you
without fear of successful contradiction, and
that is that no people similarly situated have
ever made the progress in every department of
life that our people have made, since the world
began. Why, just think of it! Twenty-seven
years ago we did not own a foot of land, not a
cottage in this wilderness, not a house, not
a church, not a school-house, not even a name.
We had no marriage-tie, not a legal family—
nothing but the public highways, closely
guarded by black laws and vagrancy laws, upon
which to stand. But to-day we have two
millions of our children in school, we have
about eighteen thousand colored professors

and teachers, twenty thousand young men and women in schools of higher grade, two hundred newspapers, over two million members in the Methodist and Baptist Churches alone, and we own over three hundred million dollars' worth of property in this Southern country. Over a million and a half of our people can now read and write. We are crowding the bar, the pulpit, and all the trades, and every avenue of civilized life, and doing credit to the age in which we live.

"I tell you, madam, I am not much disturbed about our future. True, I cannot and do not pretend to be able to solve the negro problem, as it is called, because I do not know that there is really such a problem. To my mind it is all a matter of condition and national and constitutional authority. Get the conditions right, and my faith is that the natural functions, security to 'life, liberty, and happiness,' will follow. My advice to my people is: 'Save your earnings, get homes, educate your children, build up character, obey the laws of your country, serve God, protest against injustice like manly and reasonable men, exercise every constitutional right every time you may lawfully and peacefully do so, and leave results pal Church. God's plan seems to be to pattern this country after heaven. He is bringing here all nations, kindreds, and tongues of people and mixing them into one homogeneous whole; and I do not believe we should seek to frustrate his plan by any vain attempts to colonize ourselves in any corner to ourselves."

With this the colonel left, expressing himself delighted with his visit, as I am sure I was.

11

CHAPTER XIX.

THE COLORED DELEGATES.

The General Conference of the Methodist Episcopal Church,
1888—Negro delegates—Reception tendered them by
Mrs. General Grant—Presentation of a Bible to Mrs.
Grant—Dr. Minor's great presentation address.

THE following year, during the month of
May, I visited the General Conference of
the Methodist Episcopal Church, which was
then in session in the city of New York. It
was the most representative body I had ever
met in my life. There were representatives
there from every State and Territory in the
United States, from all parts of North and
South America, and from Europe, Asia, Africa,
and the isles of the sea.

In that assembly were also fifty-three colored
delegates, sandwiched promiscuously every-
where like so much black pepper in a vessel of
salt. They took part in all the deliberations
of the Conference, and were received every-
where with the utmost cordiality. Some of
them acted as secretaries of the general body ;

others were secretaries of committees, while
they were represented on all the great committees, special and standing, of that body.
They were an excellent body of men, and represented their constituencies with becoming
dignity and character. I really felt proud of
them. But I want to tell you of an incident
which took place while I was there, and to
which I was permitted to be a witness.

Mrs. General U. S. Grant prepared and extended a grand reception, in her palatial man-
sion, to the colored delegates in the Conference. Among her invited guests, besides the
delegates and such of their families and friends
as accompanied them, were General John
Eaton, ex-United States Commissioner of
Education; United States Senator Leland
Stanford, the millionaire senator from California, and wife; Bishop and Mrs. John F.
Hurst, Bishop and Mrs. John P. Newman, and
other distinguished guests. Then there were
also present her son, Colonel Fred. D. Grant,
now United States Minister to Austria, and
wife, and several of her grandchildren. The
ladies here mentioned received with the Grant
family. The delegates manifested their ap-

preciation by purchasing a beautiful Bagster Bible, which was presented to Mrs. Grant as a token of their esteem. The gentleman selected to make the presentation address was introduced to Mrs. Grant and proceeded to deliver his address, to the delight of all present.

But who do you suppose he was? Why, bless you! it proved to be no other than the Rev. Dr. Daniel Minor, the son of Uncle Jacob Turner, one of Uncle Cephas's fellow-servants, who was willed free by his master, but who was sold in Tennessee at the same time that Uncle Cephas was sold. Dr. Minor was sold from his father when he was only six years old; so he was raised by his master, who gave him the name of Dan Minor. But I tell you, his speech was a real masterpiece of polished eloquence, and was delivered with such marked effect as to charm, subdue, and bring forth tears from many that stood and heard it. I know you would have been glad to have been there and to have heard it; so I shall try to repeat it for you. Said he:

" Mrs. General Grant, the colored delegates to the General Conference of the Methodist he returned to his native land our arms and hearts were exultantly opened wide for his reception. Our admiration and joy knew no bound, and all the powers behind the throne could not resist us in our efforts to have him honored with the presidency for a third term. If his friends failed in their attempt, we have the proud satisfaction of knowing that our race never faltered in his support. . . . When General Grant visited my native State, on his return from the Orientals, I had the distinguished honor and pleasure of delivering to him an address of welcome in behalf of the colored ministers of our city, in the course of which I called his attention to an incident which had recently taken place in Florida; and I take pleasure in repeating it now to you. At a certain hotel there many of our people called to see and pay their respects to him. The proprietor of the hotel in question was offensively affected by their presence, and sought to drive them away. Did General Grant tamely submit to the harsh and inhuman treatment about to be visited upon us? No; said he, ' Let them come in, for where I am, there they may come also; if not at this, then at some other hotel.' This, to us, is one of the most precious treasures that we have inherited from him.

" During the long, weary months of his terrible affliction many sympathizing hearts with tearful eyes watched the daily bulletins giving account of his wonderful struggles between life and death. The nations had their fingers on his pulse. They counted his breathing, watched his temperature, dwelt upon every change in his diet, appetite, strength, and treatment. When the summons came, and he that had never lost a battle went down beneath the conquering hand of death, leaving your heart and home in desolation, a cry of lamentation went up throughout the land. Messages of sympathy and condolence poured in upon you from the palaces of the rich and the hovels of the poor, from every State in this country and from many of the crowned heads of other lands; but we can assure you that no hearts were more deeply wounded, no eyes wept more bitterly, and no mourners were more genuine than those of the people we represent. They, of all the people, next to yourself and immediate family, sustained the greatest loss and experienced the greatest pain.

"Our only comfort came from the knowledge that, through the blessed Gospel which we preach, he had conquered death, and from the knowledge that he had been spared to complete his great book which would make his dear family comfortable. With no mass of wealth at our command, we have not been able to embody our devotion to him in marble or in brass; but, purer and more precious and enduring than the purest marble or the costliest brass, he has, by his own deeds, established in our heart of hearts a throne of power which all the flames and floods of all the succeeding ages can never destroy or impair.

"And now, as a token of our love and eternal devotion to his sacred memory, and of our alliance to his family, we beg you to accept this token, this Holy Book, which General Grant called the sheet-anchor of our liberties; this Holy Book, which teaches us our relation to God as our Father, man as our brother, and which fits us for holy living and prepares us for happy dying. Accept it as the pledge of our devotion to his memory, to yourself, and to all your dear ones."

Now, wasn't that a grand speech? And

then to think that such a man was once a poor, down-trodden slave! I tell you, there must be hope for a race that can produce such men in such a short length of time and with such limited opportunities.

Bishop Newman then responded, in behalf of the family, in a very excellent address, which all greatly enjoyed. The delegates and other invited guests were then ushered into the capacious and brilliantly lighted dining-room, where all the choicest delicacies of the season were served them by the distinguished ladies that assisted Mrs. Grant in the offices of the occasion. The many valuable and rare treasures and mementoes presented to the general by princes and potentates of foreign lands were then shown the visitors. An hour or more was spent in the most pleasant recital of reminiscences of the general's attitude toward the colored people, during and since the war, by General Eaton, Bishop Newman, and others; and the delightful and memorable affair passed into history. I need not tell you that I enjoyed the occasion. Who would not?

CHAPTER XX.

A TOUCHING INCIDENT.

The Cotton Centennial Exposition of 1884—Dr. Lee's great
speech—Aunt Jane Lee finds her long-lost son—The
reunion.

I CANNOT close my story until I tell you
of a very touching incident which I can
never forget, which took place about four
years before that which I have just related.
I know you will enjoy it, and therefore I don't
feel that it is necessary for me to make any
further apology for going back to recall it.
The incident took place during the great Cotton Centennial Exposition which was held
in New Orleans in 1884. It was one of the
finest and most extensive ever witnessed in
any country. On one of the many special
days that were observed there I had the
pleasure of listening to many very eloquent
and gifted orators, and among them was a
young colored man who was said to have been
a slave, and who was to speak as the representative of his race. The programme was a

long and tedious one, and the people grew tired and restless; but of the sixty thousand people that had gathered nearly all remained to the last in order to get a chance to hear the colored man that would dare attempt to interest such a concourse of people after so many able orators had almost nauseated them with the choicest flower of classical oratory. At the appointed time, however, he made his appearance and was introduced. Although there were nearly sixty thousand people present when he uttered his first sentence you could almost have heard a pin drop, so intent was every one to hear what he would say. To say that he acquitted himself creditably but feebly expresses the fact. He did so well that not only the local press, but the press of the whole country, echoed his praise to the very skies. Indeed, he surprised the nation. Describing the occasion in *Harper's Magazine*, that matchless writer, Charles Dudley Warner, said:

"The colored citizens took their full share of the parade and the honors. Their societies marched with the others, and the races mingled on the grounds in unconscious equality of privileges. Speeches were made glorifying

the matter, only to unite. in praise to God for
the wonderful reunion that he had thus vouch-
safed to this long-separated mother and son.
I almost felt that I was one of the family,
too, for Aunt Charlotte had told me so many
things about Aunt Jane Lee; and now that I
was permitted to form her acquaintance under
such circumstances I could not restrain my
tears nor my joy. I then took them to my
house, which was only a few squares away,
where I listened to them as they recited to
each other the wonderful story of their lives
during the years of their separation.

After spending nearly half the night with
me and my family and friends who had gathered to witness this affecting scene we all
united in singing, " Praise God, from whom all
blessings flow," after which Dr. Lee led in
prayer, and the company separated, and Dr.
Lee and his mother left, with the promise
that they would soon write. Dr. Lee was well
situated in life. He had managed to work his
way through college, had amassed a considerable amount of property, had married a very
excellent wife, a former school-mate, and had
one daughter; and now he was going to com-

plete his family circle by the addition of his long-lost mother, who was going to accompany him to his comfortable and cultured home in Baton Rouge.

But when will all this scattered race be re-united that was thus most cruelly separated by our inhuman system of slavery? Never, till they gather before the throne of God, when all nations, great and small, shall then be called to their final account. Let us all thank God and rejoice that the unearthly institution has been swept away forever in a sea of blood never to rise again.

"Sound the loud timbrel o'er Egypt's dark sea;
Jehovah has triumphed, his people are free!
Sing, for the pride of this tyrant is broken,
　His chariots, his horsemen, all splendid and brave—
How void was their boast, for the Lord hath but spoken
　And chariot and horsemen are sunk in the wave.
Sound the loud timbrel o'er Egypt's dark sea;
Jehovah has triumphed, his people are free!

Praise to the Conqueror, praise to the Lord!
His word was our arrow, his breath was our sword.
Who shall return to tell Egypt the story
　Of those she sent forth in the hour of her pride?
For the Lord hath looked out from his pillar of glory,
　And all the brave thousands are dashed in the tide.
Sound the loud timbrel o'er Egypt's dark sea;
Jehovah has triumphed, his people are free!"